## Critics Praise

From *The Washingt[on]*
*[This book] is an a[uthor]...*
Miller's enthusiasm and total enjoyment in the lessons she learned. The author, a psychotherapist, uses her garden for spiritual renewal, to better understand life and as a place to meditate and feel a connectedness with all that we have on earth. The 163-page hardback is a good read and will have your total focus.
  —Joel M. Lerner

From *Washington Woman*
Local author Dr. Alice Miller shares her experiences planning, planting and nurturing a woodland garden in her book . . . . With laughter, prayer, grace and faith, Miller shows how garden paths can be a metaphor for life and how our earthly environment is a sacred trust to be preserved for future generations. Curl up with this heartwarming book . . . when you find yourself longing for springtime.
  —Alicia Brewster

From *The Potomac Gazette*
  Alice Miller, a psychotherapist . . . has just merged two paths . . . the spiritual insights from her life experiences and the creation of a woodlands garden.
  And, a garden, as Alice demonstrates in her book, mirrors life — its losses, its growth, its changes — blooming where we are planted, and sometimes blooming where we least expect it.
  She has planted in her pages quotations and poems that enrich the conversation she has with her readers, including one that reminds me of the season we are about to enter, which I label the "when-will-winter-end season."
  ...From conflict and death to joy and birth, Alice's garden has been there for her. And, as she observes in her final passage, "As the steward of my garden, I have nurtured it. And so, also, has the garden nurtured me."
  Now, she shares her garden with us.
  —Chuck Lyons

# TO EVERYTHING
# THERE IS A SEASON

*May the spirit of the garden be with you*

*Alice H. Miller*

# To Everything There is a Season

## A Psychotherapist's Spiritual Journey Through the Garden

### Dr. Alice G. Miller

SEABOARD PRESS

AN IMPRINT OF J. A. ROCK & CO., PUBLISHERS

*To Everything There is a Season*  Dr. Alice G. Miller

SEABOARD PRESS

is an imprint of *JAMES A. ROCK & CO., PUBLISHERS*

*To Everything There is a Season* copyright © 2005, 2007
by Alice G. Miller

*Address comments and inquiries to:*
SEABOARD PRESS
9710 Traville Gateway Drive, #305
Rockville, MD 20850

**E-mail:**
jrock@rockpublishing.com    lrock@rockpublishing.com
Internet URL: www.rockpublishing.com

Trade Paperback ISBN: 1-59663-784-6 / 978-1-59663-784-9

Library of Congress Control Number: 2006937873

Printed in the United States of America

First Printing: 2007

*This book is dedicated to
my husband, lover and best friend,
Stan Miller – who will always be
the Adam in my Eden.*

## Acknowledgements

I am deeply grateful to Roy Howard, my pastor, friend and spiritual inspiration. As my writing coach, Roy has read and re-read many of these pages and offered insight and encouragement. Thank you. Thank you. Thank you.

And thanks to my dear friends at Saint Mark Presbyterian Church, a community of inspiration and support who have always been there for me throughout the years.

For Jim Macdonell, Pastor Emeritus of Saint Mark, who has been my friend since the beginning. From Selma, Alabama to Belfast, Ireland, he continues to live his vision of the social gospel that shaped a church.

To Ruth Helvenston, kind friend and mentor as I made my journey from student volunteer to professional. I will never forget the many words of support and wisdom, always offered with a twinkle.

And thanks, finally, to the Chevy Chase Presbyterian Church, my first church home. They provided the beginning step in my spiritual journey when they welcomed a little girl from outside the community. Each week I was brought to Sunday School by a church family, and then to the Fireside Youth Group which touched so many lives.

Like the parable of "The Sower and the Seed," churches often do not know whose lives they deeply touch. Nor do they always get thanked. Unless, of course, you believe that the greatest thanks is love passed on.

—A.G.M.

# TABLE OF CONTENTS

# Introduction

This is not the book I started to write. That book was about a psychotherapist who found a haven in her garden and decided to write a "how-to" for someone who, like herself, would like to create a place of beauty, but has no technical knowledge – and knows the Latin name of nothing. Actually, I know two Latin names: taxus repandens (spreading yew) and tierella cordifolia (foam flower).

But, for me, writing a book is a little like making a garden, which itself is a little like life. You can't just superimpose your own master plan. Life and books and gardens are, as John Lennon said, what happens while you are making other plans.

Somewhere along the way this book started writing itself. That is because the real story of the garden is, for me, in another dimension. I have become increasingly aware that when I leave my home office and enter the garden I have crossed over a threshold and into a sacred space. It is no more than fifteen feet from the sunroom door. It is sanctuary.

This book ended up being less about horticulture and more about sanctuary. So, if you want a book about horticulture, close the cover very carefully, avoid getting any fingerprints on the pages and hurry back to the bookstore. You may still be able to get a refund.

This is a story about garden paths – themselves a metaphor for life. It is the story of my walks down the garden path, and the stops along the way, to touch the earth and to wonder at the process. When you are a gardener you become a part of that process.

There is a garden within each of us, waiting to happen. The garden itself mirrors life.

It is loss.

It is growth.

It is change.

It is bloom where you are planted.

It is bloom where you least expected it.

But always, amid the change – a garden is growth. You cannot have a garden and not believe in tomorrow. You plant a seed, and it bursts into plant. That's not quite on a par with childbirth – but it is right up there; and it doesn't hurt as much.

So the "how-to" book I started to write has evolved into the story of a spiritual garden, which is really quite a simple concept. It is a place to retreat from the outside world of cell phones and palm pilots into a peaceful world of quiet creation. The symbolic act of walking through the garden gate and becoming at one with the garden can introduce a quieting within each of us. It is this quieting that opens the door to meditation and spiritual awakening.

When you become the steward of a spiritual garden you are doing more than just planting and weeding and watering. You are becoming immersed in the process of life, and the growing realization of your own oneness with the earth. You get to watch things come alive and to feel a part of creation. You can't do this and not believe in God.

Garden writers have often referred to this experience as the "Green Cathedral." Expressed quite simply, they see gardening as a ritual in which the garden merges with the life of the spirit.

"The garden is a sensual ritual in which the spiritual life emerges directly out of the dirt and the green and brilliant colors of nature."

I once presented this philosophy to a former pastor, when he chided me that I was missing a lot of church that summer. "But," I protested, "I was in the Green Cathedral." That one didn't fly.

But it flies for me. There is a significant part of my own faith journey that has more of a mystical quality than a structured religious quality. In fact, this rather describes me. I am a deeply spiritual person, but not a very religious person. I am a gardener and, to me, the garden is a holy place. This, of course, is in addition to, and not instead of, the church community, which for me is also about a growing spiritual life with others who share the journey. For me, I need the "Community of Saints." That is, if you include the old description of the difference between saints and sinners being only that "the saints are trying."

As a psychotherapist I deal with other people's sadness and stress. For me it is not so much the stress as the intensity of walking with others on their journey. This is not a completely detached experience, (contrary to what they teach you in graduate school.)

Therapy is not about changing other people. It is about being with them as a catalyst for their own changes as they become the person they were meant to be. Along the way that can mean pain, tears, laughter, and sometimes joy. But the walk with them can be intense. So when I have a break between clients I go into the garden, where there is always peace, no matter what else is happening in my life. And there I am healed.

Because I am fortunate enough to have an office in my home I can schedule breaks between client hours. Then I can move from the rhythm of the therapy hour and into the rhythm of the garden, where nature's Prozac is always at work.

That is the beauty of the garden. You can walk down the paths feeling a bit tattered, and the next thing you know you are smearing a little bit of peanut butter on a tree stump for the birds, and checking the pond for tadpoles. Maybe there will be a few blossoms to pick. Suddenly an hour has passed, and you are feeling relaxed, refreshed and brand new.

With all this beauty it is sometimes difficult not to be overwhelmed by my own grandiosity. I know that as a gardener you are not exactly the creator of all this beauty. You are the steward and you nurture it. On the other hand, a part of me remembers the old gardeners' story.

An old gardener moved into an aging house with a seedy, ramshackle yard filled with weeds and debris. Because he is a gardener at heart he cleans and clears and sweats and plants. Eventually, after many months of sweat and labor, the old man is able to bask in his own little Eden, filled with lush flowers and plantings.

Then along comes the good Christian who, of course, has to remind the old gardener that this is indeed a magnificent part of God's creation. "You are truly blessed," says the Christian, "that God has worked with you to make this paradise."

"Well, yeah," replied the gardener. "But you should have seen it when God had it by Himself."

Nonetheless, I am willing to give God some credit. If I didn't, the garden would remind me. It is always about life and death — birth and re-birth. There will always be beginnings and endings. You never "master" the garden. You only evolve with it. The storms, the droughts, the sun, the freezing rain, the raccoons, the moles, and God forbid, the slugs.

It is an endless cycle. That is why this book will take you through the seasons. It is not just about spring, summer, fall and winter. Rather, it is spring, summer, fall, winter and spring again. That is the cycle of birth, growth, death, and re-birth. That is what the garden teaches you. The Bible says something about this, too.

E. B. White touches on this theme in a wonderful forward he wrote for his wife Katherine's book, *Onward and Upward in the Garden.*

He writes that she would sit with a clipboard during her last fall, oblivious to her own mortality "calmly plotting the resurrection" of the coming spring.

You see there is no end — only new beginnings. The garden, in the larger sense, was here before us, and will be here after we leave this world. Hopefully, as stewards of the earth, we will leave it a little better place.

This is my story, being the steward of my garden. It is my hope that as you follow the path of this garden you will find yourself dreaming of your own garden journey.

*. . . and a time for*
*every purpose under heaven*

CHAPTER 1

# *To Everything There Is a Season*

*To everything there is a season, and a time for every purpose*
*under heaven:*
*A time to be born, and a time to die, a time to plant, and a*
*time to pluck up that which is planted;*
*A time to kill, and a time to heal; a time to break down, and a*
*time to build up.*
*A time to weep, and a time to laugh, a time to mourn and a*
*time to dance;*
*A time to cast away stones, and a time to gather stones together,*
*a time to embrace, and a time to refrain from embracing.*
*A time to get, and a time to lose; a time to keep, and a time to*
*cast away;*
*A time to rend, and time to sew; a time to keep silence, and a*
*time to speak;*
*A time to love, and a time to hate; a time of war, and a time of*
*peace.*
　　—Ecclesiastes 3:1-8

The search for our own Eden sometimes begins in our childhood. We just don't recognize it. Often it is the memories of those early years that evoke the strong feelings to which we respond much later in life. From the gardens of our childhood many of us still remember the feelings of peace, harmony and sanctuary. Now, many years later, we long to re-create a piece of that in our lives today.

For a child, that first garden may be just a secret place beneath the sheltering branches of a large tree or shrub. There they can enjoy the nurturing comfort of time along with special friends in their own secret place, or just be safe in the sanctuary of their own little piece of the earth. Years later the fond memory of that secret place will still remain:

> *Eden is that old-fashioned House*
> *We dwell in every day*
> *Without suspecting our abode*
> *Until we drive away.*
>
> *How fair on looking back, the Day*
> *We sauntered from the Door —*
> *Unconscious our returning,*
> *But discover it no more.*
> *—Emily Dickinson*

The first secret garden of my childhood was under a big, spreading spirea bush at the edge of our small Boston garden. There was always shelter to be found under the long, delicate branches. This was my special place of sanctuary and comfort.

As a little girl, I learned very quickly what many children before me have also had to learn. In some families the wrath of an angry father is a good thing to avoid. And what better place to hide than the garden.

"You were always such a little willow-the-wisp," my father reminisced years later. "You used to disappear like magic, and I could never find you." Well, that's because he didn't look under the spirea bush at the end of the driveway.

In the spring my sanctuary became a dazzling, shimmering white bridal wreath of blossoms, confirming that once again the harsh Boston Winter was really over and Spring was here to stay. Nestled safely under the branches, it felt like being in heaven, enveloped in masses of fluffy white blooms.

It was in the Springtime of my fifth year when Edna, my beloved babysitter, moved away. She had been with me ever since I could remem-

ber. It was Edna who gave me hugs and kisses and showered me with love. Whenever I picture Edna now, I am always sitting on her lap. And I am always smiling.

When Edna drove in the driveway the last time to say her final goodbye, I was so overcome with grief and loss I could not even say "goodbye." Trying to pretend that I didn't really care, I just stood there, eyes brimming over, silently shaking the branches of the old spirea bush. As all around me the soft, white petals fluttered to the ground, I could only stand, rooted to the earth and unable to speak. Instead, the soft petals spoke for me

Sometimes now, as a psychotherapist, I hear a client say, "It doesn't really hurt, and I don't care anyway," I remember the little girl under the spirea bush.

Last year we planted our own spirea bush on the path to the butterfly garden. And every time I pass it, it makes me smile at the grateful memory of the young woman I loved so much.

A few years later in another state and another garden I learned to love the grassy plot and rolling hills of our Maryland home. My brother, Dana and I staked out the two recessed stone archways in the steeply terraced backyard. There we created our own children's kingdom, surrounded by mossy rocks and ferns. And another peaceful Eden was created.

My father, who never did anything halfway, became enamored with yellow cosmos. One summer he planted a multitude of cosmos on the sunny back terraces which surrounded our stone archways. The following summers he planted hundreds more cosmos which he had harvested from the seeds of previous years. Soon the entire backyard was a glowing mass of gold.

In some ways, it was so unlike my father, who was often an angry, withdrawn man to have created a wild and random blaze of color all summer. Perhaps that is who he really wanted to be. For me, that sunny backyard was always a place of joy. It was like being warmed by a thousand tiny suns.

The real Eden dream started for me when I was in second grade and went to Saint Michael's Catholic School. My parents were "nominal" protestants, but they both concurred that for providing a child with a good moral background, you just can't beat a Catholic school education.

My father, ever the skeptic, prepared me for this experience with his skewed view that "the Catholic religion is really just a lot of mumbo-jumbo." I was there only to get a good education and to be a "good girl," whatever that meant. Unfortunately, no one ever informed me that it might be wiser not to repeat my father's religious views. Especially not at Saint Michael's where some of the "brides of Christ" were short on joy and long on righteousness. In fairness to the hardworking sisters, it was not always easy having the child of nonbelievers in class.

During the first week at Saint Michael's, I shared with a few class-mates my father's view that "holy water isn't really holy. It is just plain old faucet water that some man in a long dress mumbles over." The "news" spread rapidly. Soon I found myself pulled from my desk in the firm grip of sister Ellen Marie, who hauled me to the front of the class and sternly announced:

"We must all remember not to listen to Alice, because . . . , well . . . , uh, . . . after all," (she enunciated each word carefully, so no one would miss the shame of it all.) "Alice is a prot-es-tant!" I wasn't sure what a protestant was, but I knew it was something bad. Second grade was not a good year.

Reflecting on my year as the class leper I am left to wonder why it is that people who proclaim the love of God can sometimes be so hateful? Perhaps it is because they haven't experienced it. I did learn a lot about heaven and hell that year. Especially the latter, and who the candidates were. Because heaven, explained the sister, is a place where *only* the "just" are rewarded, and the good boys and girls get whatever they want. Wow!

"Even roller skates?" I asked.

"Even roller skates," she promised, "—for the *good* kids." It was all too clear who would not be a candidate for roller skates. Later in life, when I actually read the Bible, I could never find the part that mentioned roller skates.

Sister Ellen Marie did have a few choice anecdotes about the road to Hell, which was apparently quite well populated. The whole problem started in the garden of Eden, she explained, when Adam and Eve had to go and mess it up for everyone else. For years I assumed that Adam and Eve must have been Protestants.

What I got out of second grade was not exactly what Sister Ellen Marie had in mind. I did know that the garden of Eden sounded pretty cool. Eventually, I began to consider the possibility that Sister Ellen Marie might not have been completely accurate.

Hell, I have concluded, is not some blazing inferno filled with burning Protestants. Hell is separation from God. And that is not God's choice.

How much more joyous Sister's life, and the lives of her students, might have been had she actually been able to experience and share the good news that God's love includes everyone, even "bad" boys and girls. And that even after leaving the garden of Eden we can still find our own peace.

Indeed, we can all find the path to our own Eden. Even Protestants.

# CHAPTER 2

# *A Time to Embrace*

*God has created a new day
Silver and green and gold
Let us live that the sunset may find us
Worthy His gifts to hold.*

hose were the words to the grace before each breakfast at the Fresh Air Camp. Eight little girls from Baltimore's inner city taught me what those words mean. And we taught each other what it means to approach the earth with reverence.

Little did I know that this sun-filled grassy campus, dotted with the occasional tree and surrounded by woodland, would become a garden for my own growth. This was the summer that I would begin to understand gratitude.

It all started at the end of my senior year in high school. At the time it seemed like a lark to sign up as a junior counselor of the Fresh Air Camp to provide a nature experience for the children from the poorest sections of Baltimore City, whose only outdoor experience had been on asphalt and concrete.

Some of these children were from loving families who suffered from the relentless pressures of grinding poverty. Others were even less fortunate and had endured the daily abuse of families who suffered not only financial poverty, but also, a deeper poverty of the spirit.

Never did it occur to me that as a spoiled, privileged child of suburbia, with no training whatsoever, I might have a little difficulty dealing with a cabin full of girls, not that much younger than myself, who were

*Clematis*

growing up on the street. After all, I would be under the direction of a trained senior counselor with lots of experience.

It was not until I arrived, unpacked and settled in my cabin to await the first busload of campers, that I was notified that the senior counselor had failed to show up. In the space of a few minutes I discovered that I had just been given a field promotion. I was now the senior, and only, counselor for my cabin of eight 8-year-old girls. Uh. Oh.

The first half hour was the hardest. When the girls came bounding into the cabin I had a moment of panic wondering how I could fake "senior counselor." The reflection time was short-lived, for suddenly one of the girls drew a knife from her backpack and threw it, blade first, to the floor.

"Oh, gee, I'm going to have to put that away," I said, taking the knife. "It makes me nervous." Then we all got to the business of getting to know each other. In the process I realized that these girls had never had a counselor. However I chose to act, the girls would just assume that was what counselors were supposed to do. How hard can that be? Now, much later, I realize that the responsibility was awesome.

In one of life's little ironies, that experience was repeated many years later. This time, as a seasoned psychotherapist in a psychiatric group practice. I went to greet my new client in the waiting room. His unwashed, stringy hair was long, but not long enough to hide the message "fuck you!" emblazoned in giant red letters across the front of his dirty t-shirt. Upon entering my office he withdrew a large knife from his belt and slung it, blade down, to the floor, where it stuck, quivering through the carpet. This was a little scarier than the Fresh Air Camp. Bill's court record had already predicted that.

"I'm going to have to take that," I said, removing the knife and putting it away. "It makes me uncomfortable." I didn't say "gee" this time. Then again, this time I really did know what I was doing. That was the first of several sessions that each started with a litany about the injustice of being forced into therapy, and a list of all the things in the world that "sucked," starting with therapy. I listened.

Soon Bill began appearing in the waiting room ten minutes early for his session. Other patients in the waiting room were not overjoyed by his appearance, or his t-shirt. Eventually, Bill was able to be more explicit about what "sucked." I listened, and indeed it did. After a while he stopped wearing that t-shirt.

Getting to know my campers at Fresh Air Camp was a lot quicker and easier. They came with an exuberance and a capacity for joy that had not yet been dimmed by a hard life.

For most, it was their first experience with rolling green hills and woodland, and air free from exhaust fumes. As the thin veneer of toughness dropped away, it was replaced with the sweetness and laughter of eight little girls who were awakening to the sheer joy of being alive and experiencing all the earth had to offer.

Ralph Waldo Emerson would have loved being with my girls and seeing their enthusiasm. He once commented that if the appearance of the constellations only occurred every Millennium, it would be touted as a thrilling event. But they appear every night. So who looks?

That summer I was given a chance to see through my Camper's eyes what I had always taken for granted. And I passed it back to them. We touched the trees together, and laughed, and rolled down hills. There were daisy chains to make, wreathes for our hair, and all the green to run barefoot through. Those eight little girls showed me the earth's beauty anew and I showed them theirs.

That old hymn, "For the Beauty of the Earth," could have been written for the Fresh Air Campers:

> *For the Beauty of the earth,*
> *For the glory of the skies*
> *For the love which from our birth,*
> *Over and around us lies.*
> *Lord of all to Thee we raise,*
> *This our hymn of grateful praise.*

*For the wonder of each hour*
*Of the day and of the night,*
*Hill and vale and tree and flower,*
*Sun and Moon and Stars of Lights,*
*Lord of all to Thee we raise*
*This our hymn of grateful praise.*

Although life had been tough for some of these children, there was never any shortage of laughter and hugs. Sadly, some of the girls arrived with bad cases of impetigo. The camp nurse quickly decorated the infected areas with large splotches of bright purple gentian violet medication.

Throughout the campgrounds appeared the occasional purple dotted camper, painfully trying to hide the telltale stains of shame. The counselors and the other campers were all informed by the nurse that impetigo came from 'filthy living conditions." And was highly contagious. Everyone was told to avoid all physical contact with the infected children. Soon the purple splotches became a symbol as powerful as the leper's bell.

Avoiding physical contact was fine in theory, but what of little Doris, shy and sad and covered in purple blotches, who sat silently watching whenever another child was roughhousing or being hugged?

One afternoon in the final days of camp we were all sitting on the grass weaving daisy chains. Doris came over to where I was sitting and quietly crawled into my lap and put her arms around me. She laid her head on my shoulder and sighed. There is only one way this story could end. Two weeks later I started my freshman year in college sporting one very purple left ear.

It must have rained that summer, but I can only remember the endless sunny days. The campers seemed never to tire of running through the camp, feeling the grass under their bare feet, or playing countless games that all seemed to involve singing and going round and round in circles.

The camp favorite was Punchenella, an old standby, to be played while waiting for the dining room to open, a program to start, or almost anything else to happen. One lucky person got to stand in the middle of the circle while everyone else joined hands and circled around her while singing:

*What can you do, Punchenella-funny-fella?*
*What can you do, Punchenella-funny-do?*

At which point the child in the center would do some wild movements consisting of multiple leaps, turns and twists. Then the campers would continue to circle her while singing at the top of their lungs:

*We'll do it too, Punchenella-funny-fella*
*We'll do it too, Punchenella-funny-do.*

All the children in the circle would then mimic the gyrations of the child in the center. Then came the best part. Everyone would collapse on the ground, convulsed in laughter. The worst part was that each child would then yell "me . . . me . . . now it's my turn to be Punchenella." This can get old in a hurry.

Now, all these years later, I sometimes see a broad sweep of grass, maybe bald in patches, and I remember Punchenella and all the laughter.

That summer there were lots of hugs and laughter for me also. I had developed close friendships with many of the counselors, met an exciting man, and watched the kids thrive in the camp experience. By August I had decided that things couldn't possibly get any better. They didn't.

One evening I was summoned to a meeting with the camp director. This would not appear to be a very threatening experience. He had always seemed to be a pleasant, but distant person. This was a man who smiled a lot, especially when he was nervous. Like now.

With his dark good looks and salt and pepper hair, the director could have been a middle-aged George Clooney look-like. Of course, George would not be likely to appear in public looking like he had been dressed by his mother, in multi-striped cotton t-shirts tucked into khaki pants. The pants sported a whole mess of little pockets up and down the legs. The clipboard and whistle around his neck didn't help either.

Sitting at his battered metal desk, fingers sharply steepled, the director smiled and eyed me quietly, while my stress level rose to new heights.

I wonder what he keeps in all those little pockets? I asked myself, trying to divert my thoughts from the implications of the lengthening silence.

"Alice," you really are a good person," he said gently.

I squirmed. This was starting to sound like the build-up for a pink slip. "You really are a good person, but . . ." Even then I knew that when the word "but" is at the end of a phrase it usually negates the first part of that phrase.

". . . But," continued the director, "I have noticed a few things." Those few things included his discovery that often my campers appeared without shoes.

Sometimes their beds were not properly made, and worst of all, their counselor was not providing "adequate" nutritional training. This to the girl who still thought that doughnuts were part of a major food group. Guilty as charged. I should have used the twinkie defense.

"Alice," sighed the director, "I have never had a counselor who loved the kids more and did less for them."

I swallowed hard and tried to look like a "real" senior counselor, while promising to work harder on nutritional skills and unmade beds. Inside, I just felt tarnished. "But," I wanted to ask, choking back tears, "what about Punchenella-funny-do?"

What indeed? Now looking back at that wonderful golden summer, I would do it all over again. Certainly nutrition is very important, I'm not so sure about unmade beds. But, if we don't first teach our children to love the earth and each other, who will?

There is more than one way to be well fed.

# CHAPTER 3

# A Time to Plant
# And a Time to Pluck up
# That Which Is Planted

*I went to the woods because I wished to live
deliberately, to front only the essential facts of life, and
see if I could not learn what it had to teach, and not,
when I came to die, discover that I had not lived.*
—*Henry David Thoreau,* Walden

hen it came time to buy our dream house I decided that, like Thoreau, I too wished to live deliberately, or moderately deliberately. No yet being the purist that Thoreau was, I longed to find an Eden where I could commune with Nature and find a spiritual retreat. But, I also preferred to continue enjoying central heat and indoor plumbing.

Eden, for me, was the fantasy of a stone house nestled in a large woodland garden. The alternative fantasy involved buying a large woodland lot and building a stone house.

"It sounds like a fantasy to me," commented by husband, Stan, who is the Adam in my Eden.

Actually, it might be better not to pursue that analogy. Then I would have to be Eve. And anyone who has ever read the Old Testament knows that Eve was a spoiled, lazy twit, who was given everything, never toiled in the garden, and then went out and stole an apple. Not to mention, one of her kids turned out rather badly, too.

So, my partner, who shall henceforth be called Stan, and not Adam, joined me in the long search for our dream house. Instead of the fantasy house, we fell in love with a long, low, red brick rambler, in the Potomac, Maryland, suburb of Washington, D.C. Sporting dark green shutters and awnings, the house evidenced every bit of its 1950's origins. "Vintage," is the term we prefer.

This was not an architecturally based decision. Our "dream house" closely resembles a red brick shoe box with shutters. But it is our house, and we love it. More accurately, we fell in love with the yard. And it was only a yard when we first saw it. The garden was yet to be.

The minute we saw the grassy back acre, dotted only with a few aging apple trees and a tired lilac, we knew it was meant to be ours. So we did not build a house in the woods. We bought the house and built the woods.

Then began a 20-year saga of planting large trees, laying circuitous brick and needle pathways, adding understory shrubs, and finding ferns and perennials to naturalize the entire area. None of this was done with any discernible order, of course.

The first step began as the "great chain saw massacre." The rotting, bee infected, old apple trees would have to go. Gnarled and decrepit as they were, the trees still produced enormous quantities of wormy, mis-shapen apples. The apples fell to the ground in droves and appeared to rot on their way to earth.

Trying vainly to collect the mushy, brown remains would result in frenzied kamikaze attacks by hordes of hostile bees, defending what was now their territory. So much for the romantic setting I had envisioned with wicker chairs and tables nestled in the shade of a spreading, old apple tree.

Oh well. The "spreading apple trees" were soon to be history. Stan had visions of himself sawing the trees to the ground. I had visions of him missing a few limbs of his own.

It was a surprise time. One morning while Stan was at work I called a local tree company. They arrived with a truck full of men, complete with assorted pieces of equipment and ladders. In a few short hours the trees were down, the debris was removed, and the newly horizontal landscape was lightly mulched.

"What happened to the trees? asked a bewildered Stan, when he arrived home that evening. I tried the "what trees?" approach, which didn't go over any better than the "maybe you were just hallucinating when you thought there were trees" approach.

It was not until much later that Stan confessed, that after the initial shock wore off, what he had actually experienced was a profound sense of relief. The whole idea of actually crawling up in all those trees with a chain saw had been rapidly losing its appeal.

I could barely contain myself waiting for the arrival of that first spring. It meant one BIG thing. It was now time to re-forest. Let the games begin.

It was indeed an unusual beginning. We wanted a forest and we wanted it now. None of this "buy 25 seedling trees and watch them grow." Not for us. When I inherited the gardening gene it didn't come with patience included. There was a solution. It appeared with the arrival of an entire truckload of very large, but very damaged trees.

The trees came from a small suburban garden center with the distinctly unbotanical name "Fat Albert's." The owner was Fat Albert, of course. I never knew why he called himself that. He wasn't fat. His name wasn't Albert. And he didn't appear to be very interested in gardening.

The twenty-plus pine, spruce and fir trees all originally had been magnificent eight-to-ten foot tall heavily branched beauties. That was before Fat Albert had jammed them all together in one small section of the garden center's lot. There they had been languishing since their arrival the previous spring. When I first spied them, huddled in the corner, they were a sad, misshapen bunch.

"Okay, guys," I greeted them. "It's time to come home." But first there was the sales dance to go through with Fat Albert.

"You are going to have a hard time selling these trees now," I pointed out. "A third of their branches are missing, and there are bald spots."

". . . And you are going to have a hard time getting a truckload of big trees for the price you want to pay," he responded. We had a lot of fun with that.

By the end of our discussion I had purchased a truckload of big trees for $10 a tree. As a bonus, Fat Albert agreed to drive them to their new home. Each tree would be placed in its own hole, he promised, provided the holes were already pre-dug and marked. We parted happily, each feeling that we had gotten the better part of that deal.

Preparing for the arrival of our new trees proved to be a bigger undertaking than I had anticipated. Armed with a hammer, stakes, plastic ribbons, and my ever-present clipboard with diagrams for the placement of each tree, we were ready to begin.

Pacing back and forth through the garden, we placed and then replaced the spot for each tree. At each prospective spot Stan hammered in a be-ribboned stake. But first there was the debate:

"How about right here?"

"No, I think a little bit to the left would be better . . . No, not that much."

"I can't do that. It won't leave enough room for the path."

"Well, let's move the path then."

"Can't do that. It will make a funny curve in the path."

"Okay, fine."

"No, wait. Let's put the fir tree in that space and put the pine tree in the back."

Try repeating this process twenty-plus times and then see what shape your marriage is in. And this was before we even got to digging the holes for the trees. Sharing the task of preparing all the holes would be a wonderful experience in togetherness. Anyway, this is the way I presented it to Stan. He proved to be a harder sell than Fat Albert.

Love being stronger than logic, he agreed to proceed with the project. Now, preparing a really good hole for any big tree, let alone these poor, battered babies, is a big job. These were going to be big root balls, and the holes would need to be twice that size.

All the extra space would be filled with rich topsoil and compost, so the roots could spread out, relax and be nourished. By the time we got to the final hole I was exhausted and whining. I wanted my clipboard back.

Beware of what you wish for. Much later, when I did have to resort to clipboard gardening it was after a disastrous experience with a 12-foot tall fir tree. I had decided to plant the tree myself, but the nursery man surprised me by arriving early. Having had no time to dig the hole, I drew an outline of the prospective hole and the nursery man obligingly plopped the tree beside the drawing.

No problem, I thought. I can just slide this baby right in. After digging my big, beautiful hole I filled it with enough water to sink in and moisten the surrounding dirt. For good measure I watered the root ball, too. This was not a smart thing to do. Now I had a huge, sodden root ball that was twice as heavy as it had been before.

This soggy ball of earth now rested at the edge of the hole. Realizing that there was no way I would be able to re-position the tree once it was in the hole, I decided that it would be quite clever to get in the hole myself and then just slowly ease in the tree. Wrong. I eased and eased, but the tree did not understand "slowly."

Suddenly, with a *plop*, the whole thousand pound (well, that's what it felt like) root ball landed on my foot. Anyhow, that is how I explained it to the orthopedist.

About now you may well be thinking that there is another reason that this is not a "how-to" book.

The fir tree is now quite beautiful, and I don't walk funny any more. So I guess it was all worth it.

It was certainly worth it the day Fat Albert arrived and began popping trees into their appropriate holes. As each tree was placed we removed its dead branches and adjusted the tree's placement in the hole so that the gaps would be less visible. Using sturdy cords, we gently pulled the remaining branches closer together to cover the bare places. This is called tree-odonture. Okay, I made that up.

But it worked for us.

When the last tree was watered, and the last bucket of mulch was spread, Stan and I could only lean on our shovels and stare. It was a mini forest. It was awesome. Finally, we retired to the patio lounge chairs to settle down for a cold drink and some serious tree watching.

The sunshine filtered through the tree branches and already there were the soft chirps of birds, who had just discovered their new trees. You could feel the peace. It was a new world. For a brief moment it was as if we had, in some small way, become co-creators with God. I could feel the "Wow!"

I wonder if this is how God felt on the sixth day . . . and behold, it was very good.

# CHAPTER 4

# *A Time to Sow*

*Chorus:*
*Da-da-yeinu_____, da-da-yeinu_____, da-da-*
*yeinu_____.*
*dayeinu, dayeinu, dayeinu.*
*(repeat)*

*Had He given, given to us, given to us all the Sabbath,*
*then it would have been enough. Oh, dayenu.*

*Chorus:*
*Had He given, given to us, given to us all the Torah,*
*then it would have been enough. Oh, dayenu.*
*Chorus:*

 f God never did any more special favors, this favor would have been enough. So goes the theme of Dayenu, the well-loved song of Passover, the holiday that celebrates the freedom of the Jews from Egypt. Dayenu is a joyful song of thanksgiving that lists the many favors that God has bestowed upon the Jews.

Had He brought all of us out from Egypt, then it would have been enough. Oh. dayenu.

Literally, what the chorus dayenu is saying, is "it is enough." The larger meaning being, "for that alone, we should be grateful." In the context of the Passover service, dayenu is a reminder of the exodus and the message of redemption.

This is a gentle reminder that redemption means the integration of the spirit of psalms into our own life process. Indeed, this is a message that we would all do well to live by.

As a gardener it seems to me that it would also be fitting to offer up thanksgiving for today's bounty:

> *Had He given to us all the little animals, and birds and*
> *butterflies, then it would have been enough. Oh, dayenu.*
> *Had He given to us the warm sun shining in the garden beds,*
> *and lighting up the bright and beautiful tones of all the*
> *flowers, then it would have been enough. Oh, dayenu.*
> *Had he given to us the rich dappled shade of the woodland,*
> *then it would have been enough.*

Well, you get the idea.

A special "would have been enough" was fitting for our new "old" woods. By the spring following their adoption, the trees had already begun to shoot up and to fill out. The back yard had now become a woodland. It was re-named by our neighbors, who, to this day, refer to the garden as Sherwood Forest.

Soon Sherwood Forest was calling for some leafy green trees to rustle in the spring and summer breezes. In the fall they would drop hundreds — no thousands — of leaves to compost and provide nourishment for the entire garden. The new trees turned up, in what had now become the usual way, while I was making other plans.

Plans are made to be broken, or delayed. I know mine often are. For example, I am unable to resist a good yard sale. When I see that enticing sign, "yard sale," I will usually stop en route to another destination. I just can't resist the opportunity to forage for treasure.

The odds and ends of furniture, clothing, and general household discards hold little interest for me, These I will sail right past, stopping only when I get to the real treasure, the book section. However, the day is

rapidly approaching when I will have to re-think this habit. The entire
lower level of our house has now become wall-to-wall books.

It was a beautiful spring day when, driving to some long forgotten
errand, I screeched to a halt at the sign for yet another yard sale. This time
I never even got to the book section. An immediate detour was necessitated by the appearance of a large, crudely lettered sign which read: "Dogwoods 50¢ apiece. You dig them up, and you fill the hole." Oh joy!

These dogwoods were the variety that gardeners refer to as "volunteers." Usually, the volunteers have seeded themselves. They may be the
offspring of nearby parent trees, or the result of contributions deposited
by passing birds. Well, of course, I had a shovel and cardboard cartons in
the car. Doesn't everyone?

The owner's yard was dotted with these volunteers. Apparently, the
young dogwoods had been growing steadily, unattended, for several years.
Most were three or more feet tall. The owners' generosity probably arose
from the fact that they were not interested in living in Sherwood Forest.
However, in a few more years they would be.

It was a marriage made in heaven. I wanted the cheap trees. They
wanted the free labor. Sometimes things just work out that way. Much
later, with a very sore back and a car loaded with very beautiful dogwoods,
I pulled into our driveway.

Fortunately, Stan was home and went immediately into the rescue
mode with the now rapidly dehydrating trees. The shock of being so rudely
dug up from their former home, and left with precious little root ball for
nourishment, had taken its toll. The once beautiful dogwoods were now a
limp, wilted version of their former glory.

Stan made deep, compost-filled, five-dollar holes for each of our fifty-
cent trees. Some of the weaker trees were paired together in the same hole.
This would ensure that a prominent location would have one surviving
tree. If they both survived, one tree would have to be sacrificed. Or, on a
more positive note, it would be returned to the earth to provide nourishment for the garden.

Each tree was gently placed in the new hole, surrounded with rich

compost and top soil, and watered to the saturation point. In the following weeks, if nature did not provide the thirsty, young trees with a shower,
we did. Some of the trees even got a good trim so their roots would not
have to struggle to nourish extensive growth. They loved us.

Standing in awe at this beautiful new addition to our "co-creation"
woodland, I was reminded, yet again, that not all prayers are verbal. Some
are experienced deep within.

Julian of Norwich, Christian mystic and theologian, would have understood this. As a theologian, no small feat for a woman in the four-
teenth century; Julian is remembered most for her writings of a lifelong
search for a connectedness with God, and for her joyful approach to life.
With these words she might well have dedicated our garden:

> *Be a gardener.*
> *Dig a ditch*
> *toil and sweat.*
> *and turn the earth upside down*
> *and seek the deepness*
> *and water the plants in time.*
> *Continue this labor*
> *and make sweet floods to run*
> *and noble and abundant fruits*
> *to spring.*
> *Take this food and drink*
> *and carry it to God*
> *as your true worship.*
> —Julian of Norwich

As time has progressed the baby trees have grown to magnificent adult-
hood and we have been richly rewarded with a luxurious, leafy woodland
at the edge of the tall evergreen area. The uppermost branches have reached
across to each other and now form a thick canopy, which provides both
shade and an ever-changing filter for the sun's rays, as well as a home for
many nesting birds.

Where the branches overlap, the squirrels have created little mini highways so they can race from one tree to the next with minimum effort. So, we are not the only ones who have benefited from our labors.

Lying in the hammock under the spreading branches is sheer bliss. If "grace" means receiving from God great gifts that are more than I ever deserved, then surely I am in a state of grace.

There is nothing so peaceful as being lulled by the gentle rocking of the hammock and watching the shafts of sunlight sifting through the branches. Sometimes there is an incredible stillness, except, of course, for the occasional appearance of an airborne squirrel. I am at peace.

*Dayenu.* It would have been enough.

CHAPTER 5

# *A Time for Every Purpose Under Heaven*

*Something there is that*
*doesn't love a wall.*
  —Robert Frost, "Mending Wall"

t was time for paths. Already Stan and I were doing our daily garden tour. Armed with cups of coffee or iced tea, we strolled through the entire garden; drinking in its beauty and making future plans. It was long past time for paths.

If this garden had been planned by experts, or even just planned by the books, everything would have been done in a more ordered way. First, we would have developed a master plan, instead of superimposing a master plan along the way. The soil would have been prepared and the walkways would have been installed before the planning began.

That ordered garden would not be our garden. Instead, we did everything backwards, and loved every minute of it. Much of the planting was done first. Then, as the flow of the garden emerged, it became apparent where the paths would go. The end result was order superimposed on chaos.

Works for me.

Certainly structure is nothing to be sniffed at. When completed, the paths and walkways gave the garden its "bones." Without this framework the garden would have ended up as a hodgepodge of lovely plantings, all overlapping, but with no definition. The final result would be much like a beautiful face with no bone structure.

The brick walks we laid formed the basic structure of the garden. They were laid out in much the same squared off, orderly fashion seen in the gardens of Williamsburg. However, unlike Williamsburg, some of our paths sported a fancy little twisted turn. These turns were designed to accommodate a special tree or planting that was not about to be moved.

To anyone about to lay their own brick walks, I would say this: don't. Or, if you must, at least consult your orthopedist first.

The brick walkways were done in sections. Plan A called for having a brick supplier deliver all the bricks required for the entire job. These would be delivered in one truckload and be dumped in a very large pile at the end of our driveway. There they would sit for weeks.

We opted for Plan B. This plan entailed me and my nearly new Oldsmobile making numerous trips to a local building supply store. Wrong choice.

Once at the store I had to snag a large, flatbed cart, roll it to the nearest brick pile, and load it, one brick at a time. No smiling clerks ever emerged to help with the process.

I would have settled for an unsmiling, sullen clerk. There were a lot of them. Perhaps that is why that store is now out of business.

After being counted and checked out at the register, I had to wheel the cart to the parking lot, remove all the bricks from the cart and load them into my car. Still no smiling clerks in sight. Because this was not a fun trip I frequently overloaded the trunk, the back seat, and even part of the front seat. Often the back end would sag nearly to the ground. The Oldsmobile's, that is, not mine.

Once home, the bricks then had to be unloaded from the car and into the wheelbarrow before the bricklaying could even begin. This process was repeated so many times that ultimately the suspension in my not-so-nearly-new Oldsmobile was shot. So was mine.

To anyone who still insists on laying their own brick walks, I would say this: At least opt for Plan A.

Extending beyond the area entered by the brick walkways were a series of garden rooms, each connected to the other by a winding path of pine needle mulch. The path meandered through the meditation garden, into the butterfly garden, through the children's park and par course, and down a long winding raccoon path. Thanks to the reforesting of earlier years there has always been a ready supply of pine needles to replenish the path.

Naturalizing these areas proved to be a lot more fun than laying the bricks. The shrubs came first. Beauty was a big factor in selection. So was the creation of habitat for the birds. In addition to hydrangeas, crepe myrtles, viburnum, and rhododendrons, we added many more hollies, nandinas, and piers japonica. The birds would always have a ready supply of winter snacks.

Azaleas quickly became rampant in the garden, popping up in the beds and along many of the paths. The bulk of these azaleas were bought when both we and the garden were young. Consequently, many of the originals came from nursery off-season, "bargain basement" sales.

The bargain azaleas may have started out a little raggedy, but the price was right. With a little care they were soon as good as new. But what many of them did lack was little niceties like labels. To this day I have no idea what their origins may be.

Along the way I have learned the names of some of the old standbys. These azaleas are not only beautiful; they are hardy. They can be counted on to weather some of the extremes of cold, heat and drought far better than some of their fancy hybrid cousins. My favorites are: Delaware Valley White, Renee Michelle, Hershey Red, Pleasant White, and Girard's Pink.

Our woodland garden burst into life with the addition of all the understory plantings, which nestled beneath the azaleas and other shrubby plants. These are the perennials, those hardy stalwarts that remain evergreen, or after a dormant winter, return in the spring.

The garden is thick with ferns, hellebore, bleeding heart, narcissus, pulmonaria, dead nettle, euphorbia, blue phlox, and more ferns. You can never have too many ferns in a woodland garden.

Working with plants you quickly discover that in some ways they are like people. Treat them with a certain reverence and they will respond. Set them in a good home, water and nurture them and they will bloom. All this in their own time and their own way. And, like people, they don't always do what you expected, or stay where you put them. Some flourish and others need more help.

Anyone who has ever worked as a therapist, or volunteered on a mental health hotline, knows that daily they will receive a stream of phone calls echoing loneliness and despair from all walks of life. Some callers may be dysfunctional or mentally ill and require referral and ongoing treatment. But, many more are just hurting, scared, stressed, or lonely, and need a listening ear. We can all bloom a little better with some unconditional caring.

"Bloom where you are planted," does not always work with people, or with plants.

We soon learned that a master plan, while helpful, often needs to be discarded when your plants begin giving you different advice. If you listen carefully, the plants will tell you where to put them. Some of our plantings like the Christmas fern and the autumn fern seemed to settle in anywhere. Soon they were sprawling about quite happily.

Meanwhile, the Japanese painted fern squatted sullenly where she had been placed in the deep shade.

"I hate it here," the painted fern sulked. "It's too dark and too dry. See, my fronds are starting to droop."

"Okay, okay" I promised. "Things are going to get better." And they did. I picked a nice, bright moist location. The hole was filled with top soil and rotted leaves, and I gently spread out all of her little roots before watering and tamping down the dirt.

"Yes-s-s," you could almost hear her sigh as I lightly sprayed her wilted fronds. Soon the little painted fern began to perk up as she plumped out and her fronds reached for the sky.

Suddenly the garden was flourishing. Plants were bursting forth everywhere. The paths were now edged with leafy green foliage that kept spilling out into the walkways. So who needs a master plan?

On reflection, I realize that the garden has ended up a bit like me. The brick paths provide a basic order and structure. But, within those structured paths are many delightful little rooms. They are all flamboyant, overplanted, and bursting with little surprises.

Most of the understory spaces are now filled with newly propagated ferns, perennials, and wild flowers, jammed in all willy-nilly. This garden is beginning to resemble a big blowzy lady, carrying an overstuffed suitcase that bulges out on every side, with all the old bra straps hanging out.

Like me.

As the garden continued to emerge, more shady, lush and beautiful than ever, it became increasingly apparent that some form of enclosure would be necessary to complete the aura of serenity and sanctuary.

With that goal in mind, we surrounded the entire back garden with a six-foot high, wooden, stockade fence. A cedar board-on-board fence would have been more attractive.

However, our choice was determined by the difference in price, which would buy a lot more azaleas.

The result was immediately gratifying. Interestingly enough, the effect of enclosing the space actually made it appear to be much larger. It would seem that in defining the area we had now sharpened the focus on the entirety of all that was included in that space. Soon the fence was barely visible behind the rapidly spreading trees and shrubs.

Sanctuary had arrived.

It made me smile to recall Robert Burns' poem, "The Mending Wall," in which he quotes, "Good fences make good neighbors." His point being, they don't.

"You need to know what you are fencing in and what you are fencing out," says Frost.

Well, yes, I do. I am fencing out soccer balls, people taking shortcuts through my ferns, softball games, the neighbor's dogs . . . I am fencing in serenity. Just as my clients sometimes struggle with boundaries in their lives, I am aware that I also need boundaries in mine.

How ironical it was that, after writing these lines on a Saturday night, the following Sunday the sermon theme was "The Mending Wall." The focus, however, was a bit different.

"Something there is within us that doesn't love a wall," quoted the pastor. "Walls divide the world into insiders and outsiders. Walls divide people, one from the other. As Christians we are supposed to be about breaking down walls."

It sounded so right and holy when he said it. It sounded so defensive when I said, "but I *need* my enclosure."

So I find great comfort in reading the words of Henri Nouwen, Christian minister, theologian, and author of "The Wounded Healer." He speaks with compassion of the healer's ministry, and of the healer's own need for healing.

"Who," asks Nouwen, "can take away suffering without entering it?" He recounts the story from an old lesson in the Talmud:

> *Rabbi Yoshua ben Levi came upon Elijah*
> *the prophet while he was standing at the*
> *entrance of Rabbi Simeron ben Yohi's cave . . .*
> *He asked Elijah, "When will the Messiah come?"*
> *Elijah replied, "Go and ask Him yourself."*
> *"Where is He?"*
> *"Sitting at the gates of the city."*
> *"How shall I know Him?"*
> *"He is sitting among the poor covered with*
> *wounds. The others unbind their wounds*
> *at the same time and then bind them*
> *up again. But He unbinds one at a*
> *time and binds it up again, saying to*
> *Himself, 'Perhaps I shall be needed;*
> *if so, I must always be ready so as*
> *not to delay for a moment.'*

This, says Nouwen, "the Messiah sitting among the poor, binding his wounds only one at a time, always waiting for the moment He is needed," is the role of the minister. "He is called to be the wounded healer, the one who must look after his own wounds, but at the same time be prepared to heal the wounds of others." Compel-

*Bleeding Heart*

ling thought if you believe in the priesthood of all believers.

I am a long way from Messiah-hood. I am even a long way from the devotion of a Henri Nouwen. But, I do walk with people in their pain, listen with compassion, and care about them. And then, I need a garden that fills my soul. I need my walls.

After much thought on the subject, I have concluded that fences can enclose and promote sanctuary. And the garden is my sanctuary, a sacred space where I can experience peace and serenity within. Just like everyone else, I need my boundaries so I can remain open. Then from within me I can more easily let go of the symbolic fences in my life.

Still, Robert Frost was mostly right. There is something within us "that doesn't love a wall."

CHAPTER 6

# *A Time for Peace*

*Come and find the quiet Center
in the crowded life we lead,
find the room for hope to enter,
find the frame where we are freed:
Clear the chaos and the clutter,
Clear our eyes that we may see
all the things that really matter,
be at peace and simply be.*

*Silence is a friend who claims us,
Cools the heat and slows the pace,
God it is who speaks and names us,
Knows our being, touches base,
Making space within our thinking,
Lifting shades to show the sun,
raising courage when we're shrinking,
finding scope for faith begun.*
—Shirley Erena Murray
Presbyterian hymnal

The serenity of the enclosed garden is present throughout, but nowhere is it more evident than in the meditation garden.

Upon leaving the brick patio walk you turn right onto a curving path softened by a thick layer of pine needles. Here is the entry to the meditation garden. On a heavy wooden arch are inscribed the words: "Peace To All Who Enter." The message is echoed by the hanging bamboo chimes, whose gentle tones seem to be saying: "Be still and listen."

Throughout the garden we have erected similar arches to mark the entry to each different and special place. The arches are all constructed using 6x6 beams topped with a mitered edge crosspiece. Each arch bears the message of the space you are entering: the herb garden's "A Thyme to Heal," the "Children's Park," and the secluded raccoon path's message, "Breathe In, Breathe Out."

As you step through the "Peace To All Who Enter" arch of the meditation garden, the muted sounds of the bamboo chimes recede. Soon you can feel the stillness. Only the occasional bird chirps, and the steady rush of the waterfall splashing into the frog pond break the silence.

This is a place to enter quietly.

Rhododendrons, azaleas, and dogwood grow in profusion, while along the needle paths lungwort, ferns, blue phlox and wild violets creep over into the paths. In the spring the paths are dotted with narcissus, which have naturalized and pop up randomly among the rhododendrons.

This is a place to walk quietly.

This is a place to walk slowly, and to be aware of each step.

This is a place to pay attention.

In the Christian concept of "mindfulness" it is this practice of silence and paying attention where prayer is able to begin. For me, gratitude and prayer happen when I am silent and allow myself to just experience the moment. This means letting go of what Buddhists call the "monkey mind," that constant stream of internal chatter about every part of life except that part I am currently living.

The focus on paying attention to the moment is at the heart of the zen concept of "mindfulness." The word "zen" simply means "letting go. To "let go" is to be totally in the present, to live this moment fully. It is in the often quoted mantra of Ram Dass, guru of the sixties: "Be Here Now."

Thich Nhat Hanh, a Buddhist monk and zen master, refers to this quality of mindfulness in his book, "Being Peace." To illustrate this concept, Thich Nhat Hanh discusses an experience with Jim, a good friend, who was a member of the Catholic Peace Fellowship.

After sharing an evening meal with Jim and several other members of the Fellowship, Thich Nhat Hanh prepared to begin his evening ritual of washing the dishes, mindfully. This was always done before sitting down and joining the others for tea. One night Jim volunteered to do the dishes.

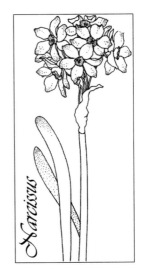

"Go ahead," responded Thich Nhat Hanh, "but if you are going to wash the dishes you must know the way to wash the dishes."

"Come on," replied Jim, "You think I don't know how to wash the dishes?"

There are two ways to wash the dishes," was the answer. "The first is to wash the dishes in order to have clean dishes, and the second is to wash the dishes in order to wash the dishes."

Jim was delighted and said, "I choose the second way — to wash the dishes to wash the dishes." From then on Jim knew how to wash the dishes. The "responsibility" was transferred to him for an entire week.

"If while washing the dishes," says Thich Nhat Hanh, "we think only of the cup of tea that awaits us, thus hurrying to get the dishes out of the way as if they were a nuisance, then we are not 'washing the dishes to wash the dishes.' What's more, we are not alive during the time we are washing the dishes. In fact, we are completely incapable of realizing the miracle of life while standing at the sink"

"If we can't wash the dishes, the chances are we won't be able to drink our tea, either. While drinking the cup of tea, we will only be thinking of other things, barely aware of the cup in our hands. Thus we are sucked away into the future — and we are incapable of actually living one minute of life."

This is how it is in the garden. If you stride down the path, thinking only about today's hurts or tomorrow's projects, then you will never truly have been in the garden.

Or, if every garden walk is only an opportunity to see what work needs to be done, then you will never completely experience all that the garden has to offer.

So, continue to follow the meditation path, and let that walk be your moment. The path weaves past a 9x15 stone-lined frog pond on the left. Only a few short years ago the pond was crystal clear and presented a stunning view of many tiny goldfish swimming in all directions over a floor of shining pebbles.

Today, however, the pond is not likely to be winning any beauty contests. Instead, beauty has taken a back seat to environmental needs. The changes occurred because the garden has always been the scene of many extended family gatherings. In order to protect the little ones it was necessary that the pond remain quite shallow.

With a depth of only 18 inches, the pond has provided the resident raccoons with their own personal wading and fishing station. Consequently, the pond bottom is frequently churned up. Mud now covers all the beautiful little pebbles. The surviving fish have learned to hide behind the larger rocks and under the stone outcroppings. Thus, they have escaped the fate of their slower siblings, who soon became hors d'oeuvres for the raccoons.

We have rewarded the valor of the survivors with a small pond heater to help them get through the cold winters. Now they have all grown fat and happy, and a different sort of beauty is emerging.

The fish have been joined by volunteer turtles and a raft of tadpoles, the progeny of the original few we purchased at a local aquarium. These newer residents love the muddy bottom of the pond. In the colder months they burrow under the mud, where they remain snoozing until the return of spring. In all likelihood, they will continue to reproduce themselves, and we will have a whole arsenal of environmentally correct, organic slug killers.

So everybody wins, except the slugs.

To the right of the pond the meditation path curves its way to the pergola. This is one of my favorite quiet spots. The overhead arbor spans an area 13x26 feet wide, and is draped with climbing hydrangea vine and autumn blooming clematis.

Fat log chairs and a small table sit on the cobblestone floor. An occasional creeping thyme appears between the cobblestones, marking the spots where the sun filters through the arbor. Sometimes, when the day is particularly clear and beautiful, I use this space for a session with a nature-loving client.

The pergola, which is both enclosed, and yet open to the sky and air, has always appeared to me as rather like a monastery colonnade. Perhaps this idea has been fostered by the presence of an almost life-sized, carved wooden statue of Saint Francis. He stands, surrounded by ferns, quietly dominating the path to the pergola.

Saint Francis has not always been with us. We spotted him one day standing at the entry to a small country antique store. His namesake, Saint Francis of Assisi, would be the patron saint of environmentalists, if they had one. They don't. So, instead, he is just the patron saint of nature and animals. Of course, we had to have him.

When he arrived he was in several pieces. His body and head were one piece. His arms and tray were separate units. In the interest of his well-being, it was decided to assemble him in the sunroom and allow him to remain there until the winter freeze was over.

Sadly for Saint Francis, he took up a considerable amount of space when he was fully assembled. His arms and tray extended into the center of the room. This left us no alternative. We removed his arms, his bird feeding tray, and the little birdies attached to his shoulder. During the entire process, he stood quietly, staring balefully at us. And there he stayed for the remainder of the winter, armless and dejected, gazing sadly out the window.

"Where is my tray?" he seemed to be asking. "Where are my little birdies? And where, for heaven sakes, are my arms?"

When March finally arrived, it was time for Saint Francis to go into the garden.

"I'm going to miss you," I whispered, as we bolted on his arms, his birdies, and his little tray. Saint Francis just kept on smiling sadly. But, I noted, he did look just a little grateful. Stan laughed. However, when the freezing rain returned that night, it was Stan who came in from the garden tour and made the announcement.

"Saint Francis hates it out there. He's cold and wet, and his feet are getting muddy. He wants to come back in." So back in he came.

When at last spring arrived, Saint Francis returned once more to the meditation garden. This time we built him a platform of cement blocks. No more muddy feet for this guy. He really did have quite attractive, lifelike feet, I noticed. The wood-carver had done a splendid job on those feet.

I briefly considered giving him a nice coat of toenail polish. Surely a man who spends all day and night barefoot deserves a good pedicure. That idea was soon to be discarded. After all, this was the meditation garden, and the good saint deserved some respect.

By this time I was becoming more aware of the value of meditation, which is really an ancient practice. In early meditation classes I learned to sit comfortably in a chair or lay prone on the floor. Quietly, with eyes shut, I began slowly to relax each muscle, going in sequence from foot to head.

In the beginning it was helpful to first tighten and then tense each muscle. Then, letting the muscles go with a slow, steady release, I was able to experience the difference between tension and relaxation.

Breathing deeply and slowly I could inhale and focus on my breath as it expanded my ribs and seemed to fill my entire body. With each slow exhale I could feel the tension drain away. Finally, my "monkey mind" was able to quiet as I continued to relax and focus on slow, steady breathing. The Western world knows this as the "relaxation response."

In meditation, one can center on a mantra, a word or words that are repeated over and over, clearing the brain of all other thoughts. Everyone must find his own mantra. Many people simply repeat the universal sound, "om." That never worked for me. It didn't feel universal or reverent. It just felt silly.

What worked for me was the Christian mantra I learned from a Jewish friend — the prayer of Saint Francis:

*Lord,*
*make me an instrument of thy peace;*
*where there is hatred, let me sow love;*
*where there is injury, pardon;*
*where there is doubt, faith;*
*where there is despair, hope;*
*where there is darkness, light;*
*and where there is sadness, joy.*

*O Divine Master,*
*grant that I may not so much seek*
*to be consoled as to console;*
*to be understood, as to understand;*
*to be loved, as to love;*
*for it is in giving that we receive,*
*it is in pardoning that we are pardoned,*
*and it is in dying that we are born*
*to eternal life.*
    —Francis of Assisi

Naturally, my Jewish friend omitted the Divine Master part. I left it in. And my old friend Saint Francis has gotten me through some tough times.

Getting through the tough times is what I first learned from my maternal grandmother, Bobbie. She was warm, loving and feisty, and she taught me how to be a strong woman.

My paternal grandmother, who insisted on being called "Grandmother," with the emphasis on the "grand," was big on control and short on empathy. My brother and I privately considered her to be the role model for the "Wicked Witch of the East." This is probably why, when my family began to expand, "Grandmother" was not a name I considered.

"Nana" was to be my grandmother name. I practiced it many times, and it always sounded quite nice. But, somewhere along the way, "Nana" morphed into "Allie," and that has been my name ever since. I like it.

Perhaps, if my paternal grandmother had lived long enough, I could have learned to like her, too. Fortunately, for both of us, she lived far away so I seldom saw her. Bobbie, on the other hand, came to visit us when my older brother was born, and never left. I know this to be a fact because my father mentioned it many times.

My parents were both agnostics, so it was Bobbie's faith that spilled over us as children. For her, God was always there, and she was always on his radar screen, a belief she passed on to us. So I was ready when my good friend, Janice, invited me to go with her to Sunday school. Every Sunday, for years, her parents drove me to Sunday school and then to youth group, and then to church.

And so a family, who cared enough to drive a little girl to church, started in motion a process that would change her life. It is like that for us all. We don't always know when some word or action of our own may deeply touch another life.

Like pebbles tossed in a pond, caring deeds produce their own ripple effect. The little girl probably never even properly thanked her benefactors. Unless, of course, you think that one of the most meaningful forms of thanks is love passed on.

By the time I was in College I "believed," but it was more of an intellectualized "thinking" belief. Sometimes I sat around wondering on a gut level what this was all about. I didn't use words like "mindfulness" and "meditation" then. In retrospect, I would just call it "listening."

It was during one of these listening times when I experienced what I now consider to be one of my life's defining moments. I had reached the "quiet center." Lacking the proper vocabulary, I can only describe the experience as a "knowing."

I knew that I was in the presence of God and I knew that God cared about me. I felt that caring. No bells and no whistles — just a sense of peace. It was that simple.

I have neither the education nor the depth to speak as a theologian. I don't have to. It is just so simple. Karl Barth, the great theologian, would probably agree with me.

*Rhododendron*

Dr. Barth, who wrote fourteen volumes of in-depth studies expounding on Christianity, was once asked by an interviewer if he could briefly summarize all fourteen volumes.

"Oh, yes," replied Dr. Barth: "Jesus loves me."

I can identify with the seminarian who wrote to the *Washington Post* in response to an article on the Trappist monk, Thomas Merton, who wrote of his spiritual odyssey in "The Seven Story Mountain." The writer said that he, too, had spent years in seminary, vainly seeking God. But, he concluded, he finally had to acknowledge what Merton had said all along. "The quest was bogus because God had found me."

That, I think, is the way it works with God. At least for me it does. I don't need to put words around it. I will carry that moment for the rest of my life.

This is the kind of prayer that I experience. I don't have the words, but I don't need them. I never pray out loud. In fact, I go to great lengths to avoid it. Listening is what I call it. For me, listening can also be what is happening when I truly feel called to do something. Then I do it. Well, usually. Sometimes I don't listen.

The listening and the quiet space that I seek in the garden is in some ways akin to the spirit of Shabbat in the Jewish faith.

Shabbat is the weekly celebration of the creation of the world and the liberation of the Jews from Egypt. From sunset Friday night until the onset of darkness on Saturday night, the observant Jews put aside the stresses and agendas of the secular world and use this time as a space apart to meditate, to renew the spiritual self, and just to love and experience a sense of joy within their world and with each other. This is to know "Shalom," the peace of God. The experience can be summed up in the Shabbat greeting and farewell: "Shabbat Shalom": Come in peace. Go in peace.

So, as you leave the winding path of the meditation garden, and walk through the exit arch, stop for a moment. Sit on the aging, pock-marked stone bench. Take in the trees all around you. Notice the delicate leaves of the nandina, "heavenly bamboo," that flank the arch. And, when you are ready, ponder the inscription carved into the heavy wooden arch.

"Shalom." Go in Peace.

CHAPTER 7

# *A Time to Seek*

*The kiss of the sun for pardon,*
*The song of the birds for mirth,*
*One is nearer God's heart in a garden,*
*than anywhere else on earth.*
—Dorothy Frances Gurney

ach path in the garden will take you through a new space of beauty. To follow the brick walk away from the meditation garden and through to the lower woodland, is to enter an arena which appears to have existed for years.

Here the brick walk gently rolls, following the swell of the earth. As a beginning bricklayer, it never occurred to me to level the path before laying the bricks. But, the end result is so pleasing that now I would not have it any other way.

Already the path appears weathered and timeless. Moss creeps around and between the bricks, which have darkened with the patina of age. The only drawback, we have since discovered, is that the patina is partially composed of grunge. Consequently, during the rainy season the grunge loosens up and the bricks quickly assume the patina of a ski slope.

Masses of red, pink and white azaleas flank the pathway. Some of them have been with us since the birth of the garden. When they burst into bloom it is breathtaking to behold.

In the spring this path becomes the most colorful spot in the garden.

43

The azaleas, having reached maturity years ago, seem quite content with the amount of light that filters through the piers japonica and dogwood that tower over them.

When I walk through the azaleas, down the old path toward the woodland, thick with ferns, I cannot help but think: "Surely this is one of God's 'thin places.'"

The early Celts believed that in the world of nature there are many "thin places." These, they believed, are the places where the membrane between heaven and earth is very thin. Here are the places where man is most closely connected with God. Here is where you will be touched by God.

How fitting it is that at the end of the azalea walk stands a weathered, gray, stone Celtic cross. The cross, which is placed amidst a pile of old rocks, is a powerful symbol of one of the tenets of Celtic Christianity: that God is connected to all things of beauty and nature.

Even during the pre-Christian era in Ireland, the Celtic pagans were deeply spiritual people. They believed in an afterlife and felt a great reverence for the world of nature.

The Roman efforts to Christianize Ireland were a dismal failure. Ultimately, Ireland's conversion to Christianity occurred in 431 AD. This was accomplished through the efforts of Saint Patrick, who was born in Roman Britain, kidnapped as a teen-ager, and brought to Ireland as a slave. After tending sheep for several years, Patrick escaped and returned to his homeland.

It is interesting that many years later the former slave would feel called to return to the country and bring Christianity to Ireland. Certainly, returning to the land of our former captors is not something that most of us would choose to do.

Unlike the missionary efforts, once so common to overzealous Christians, Saint Patrick did not abolish the pagan symbols. Instead, he merged them with the Christian symbols. The pagan stone markers were not destroyed, but marked with the sign of the cross.

The Christian cross was superimposed on the stone circle, which represented the wheel of the chariot of the sun god. The resulting cross, with arms encircled, still remains today as a symbol of Celtic Christianity.

It would appear that this came about because Saint Patrick simply told his story in both words and acts of caring. That story touched the Celtic people, who then passed it along. Pretty simple. And that is how Christianity is spread, by touching people's hearts. Not with bombs and armies.

"Bearing witness" is what the church calls this experience. But, this is not an expression that I use. I still harbor the painful memories of being the witnessee. In a period of deep searching during my college years, I connected with a small group of "devout" Christians, who had anointed themselves as the holy of holies.

Originally attracted to their strong faith, I wanted, in my vulnerability, to be just like them. They wanted me to be just like them, too. Eventually, I realized that this left no room for me to be me. The holy ones had one sole mission in life, and that was to "save" the souls of miserable sinners like myself. Whatever happened to "Jesus loves me?"

Jesus apparently got lost in the shuffle, although He sure did get talked about a lot. However, "salvation" was a full time job for the holies, as they collected the scalps of "converted" sinners to string like rosaries and hang around their righteous necks. It wasn't necessary to love the sinners, just to save them.

The more the holies prayed for me the worse I felt. I didn't want to be a miserable sinner. But, I didn't want to be "saved" by the holies either. I just wanted to smack them all. They almost "witnessed" me right out of the church. It began to feel like second grade all over again.

Ultimately, I had to leave the fold anyway. After my born-again saviors wrote reports on each of their "convert" prospects, I read the notation beside my name, which indicated that: "Alice is not really a Christian."

In response, I suggested that the real reason that the holies each wore a large gold cross on a chain around their neck was so people would know they were Christian, in case no one could tell by the way they acted. That went over big.

Of course, in retrospect, I have begun to realize that some judgment issues might apply to me as well.

There are less dramatic, and perhaps more effective ways to tell the story. Years ago, Saint Mark Presbyterian Church ran a coffee house for teens, which was a coffee house in name only. In reality, it was a loud, raucous gathering where over a hundred teens jammed into a darkened education building lit by strobe lights, and pulsating with the roar of local rock bands. This was where the action was. There were of course, those who questioned what this had to do with mission.

But, there was a different kind of action going on in the Chapel adjacent to the coffee house/education building. No one ever mentioned the Chapel, but gradually kids would drift over in twos and threes, just to sit and talk quietly. And sometimes, to talk not so quietly.

Nearly every Friday evening Dr. Warren Evans could be found sitting in the Chapel with his nose in a scientific journal. At first glance, Warren would appear to be an unlikely candidate to sit in a Chapel and talk to teenagers. A short, quiet-spoken, intellectual type, Warren was clearly brilliant and showed it.

Before long, Warren would be joined by an unruly crew, who sprawled in the pews, flicking their cigarette butts on the floor and telling some of the wildest episodes ever recounted in a sanctuary. And Warren laughed, and listened . . . and cared.

The tough guys kept coming back to see Warren. Even skeptical Don returned each week for his regular Friday night argument over the "life and death" of God. But Warren, who was extremely well read on theology, could hold his own.

"Hey, Warren, don't give me all this junk about Christian love," warned Don. "I get all that garbage at my own church. Every Monday we got religious instruction and you gotta go."

"Umm-m-m," said Warren, "You might learn something."

"Huh-h," snorted Don, "The priest that teaches us, he's always harping on love." "'You gotta love,' he says. 'You gotta love everyone.' And hell, he *hates* me."

Don had a lot of novel viewpoints. "Our church is all messed up," he declared one week. "They're always telling us what to believe and they don't even agree with each other."

"Come on, Don, you're exaggerating again," chided Warren.

"Nah-h," insisted Don, "Father Brown always hits the Catechism and says, 'You've got to believe this. If you don't live by the teaching of the church you're going to Hell!' But, Father Cross says, 'It doesn't matter what doctrine you believe. It's what's in your heart that counts.' And the Bishop just says, 'Gimme money. Gimme money.'

The next week Don returned to say that actually he didn't believe in God, anyway. "Beer is my God," he boasted.

"You have an awfully limited God," suggested Warren. "Come on in and sit down. I'd like to discuss it with you."

"Aw you're all wet!" was Don's reaction to Warren's views. "Where do you get all your dumb ideas?" And then he came in and sat down.

The next week Warren was called out of town. Don appeared in the chapel briefly, looking around in disappointment, and stomped out. Finally, after pacing past the door a few more times, Don could stand it no longer. Poking his head in the door, he demanded loudly, "Where the Hell is Warren?"

That could only happen because Warren knew that ministering to people where they are is what counts. And Don instinctively knew that he was valued just as he was. That is why he was able to listen, because he had first been listened to. Perhaps the church needs to learn to talk less and listen more.

Saint Patrick knew this. He was able to listen to the Celtic people and respect their spirituality. That is why he succeeded where the Romans had failed. Building on the deep spiritual strengths of the Celtic culture was far more powerful than attempting to destroy it. And Christianity was all the richer for connecting with a culture that helped to awaken us to the "thin place."

Like the early Celts, my mother always felt the pull of nature. She didn't worship the sun god, but she did seem to feel a deep need for connection with the living environment.

Much of her daily routine necessitated that she be inside. So, when mother was able to be outdoors, it was, for her, a huge treat. Our lawn was always dotted with striped lounge chairs and a big picnic table nestled under the trees, ready and waiting for a visitor with a spare moment.

Once outside, Mother always seemed to shed the mantle of care, and exhale a sigh of deep contentment. Now, I perceive these times in nature as a gentle letting go for her, a sense of the sacred continuum of life. But, in my early years, I would have been the last person to recognize that.

After her graduation from college, Mother had once dreamed of having an "intellectual" career that would involve literature and poetry. Instead, she married and folded her dreams into supporting her husband's career and raising her two children.

Now, when I am in the garden, I sometimes find myself thinking of my mother, a shy, gentle woman. People always liked her instantly. Friends usually described her as "soft-spoken," and "sweet." She was.

"How," someone once asked my mother, "did you ever get an outspoken, little girl like Alice?"

How indeed? What they didn't realize was that mother, who was raised in a world that valued quiet, well-mannered little girls, reveled in having a daughter who could speak up. I was her mouthpiece.

"I can't believe you said that!" Mother would admonish me with mock horror, after hearing about another outrageous remark I had made. But, the twinkle in her eye told me that she was delighted that I had said that.

Dana, my older brother, was not nearly so impressed with my wit.

"People just think you're cute now because you're little," he pointed out. "They won't think you're so cute when you're older." Usually this was followed by the observation that I wasn't all that cute now.

The only extravagant displays of emotion I ever witnessed in my mother were always centered around nature. She loved the birds and the squirrels and did her best to domesticate them. The long ledge beneath our dining room window became a giant buffet, which was constantly restocked with nuts and berries.

The squirrels spent much of their day loitering in the nearby tree branches, watching and waiting for the dining room window to open and a new offering to appear. Sometimes, as a special treat, mother would place a fat marshmallow on the ledge.

The window would barely have time to close before a squirrel would execute a flying leap from his tree branch and make a perfect four-point landing next to the marshmallow. In retrospect, I fear that a sticky, gooey marshmallow is both risky and an extremely poor nutritional choice for a squirrel.

The squirrels, however, were ecstatic. They returned the favor by remaining on the ledge to consume their new delicacy. Our favorite patron was Ralph, a large, bushy- tailed gray squirrel. Every time a marshmallow was placed on the ledge Ralph returned to repeat his routine. Comfortably settling back on his haunches, and holding the big marshmallow between his tiny, hand-like feet, he would steadily nibble away. Occasionally, the marshmallow would appear to stick to the roof of his mouth. But Ralph cheerfully persevered. He could spend an entire lunch hour trying to work his way through this mass of goo.

On the other side of the glass, we spent many lunch hours watching the birds and the squirrels. It was certainly an improvement over sharing a meal with television.

Sometimes, on lovely spring mornings, mother would arise earlier then usual. Often, in the spring months, she could be found standing in the front yard, breathing in the fresh air. "I'm drinking it in," she would announce. In those moments it was as if she truly felt a part of the sacred continuum of life.

"What a glorious day!" Mother would exalt, arms outstretched, and face skyward.

"Momm-m-m," I would groan, feeling the kind of embarrassment that only a pre-adolescent can feel. "Someone will see you."

Then, feeling the shame of it all, I would immediately retreat inside the house before I could be seen with this crazy woman. After all, I could have been ruined socially for the rest of my life.

Now I am the one standing in the garden, arms outstretched, exclaiming over the glorious day, and feeling at one with the sacred continuum of life. I wish my mother could hear me.

Maybe she can.

# CHAPTER 8

# A Time
# to Dance

*You have changed my sadness into a joyful dance;*
*You have taken away my sorrow*
*and surrounded me with joy.*
—Psalm 30:11

he joyful dance of the psalmist speaks to more than just the sheer joy of the human body in dance. It speaks to the presence and spirit of God, and the liberation of the human spirit, which can transcend suffering. And to the spirit of God, manifested in the earth. The "sacred continuum" for all who can see and feel.

Life as a sacred continuum is not a new idea. In 1984 Harvard conservation biologist, Edward O. Wilson, developed the biophilia hypotheses. Biophilia, literally, "love of life," encompasses the view that human beings have an innate connection with all aspects of the natural world, which appears to be a biologically based need.

Fulfilling this need, it is hypothesized, can affect an individual's inner harmony and physical and emotional health. Try it. Feeling stressed? Spend a lunch hour in the park, wading in a creek, or just sitting under a tree and watching the squirrels. The stressors may still be there. But you won't be in the same place. This is a survival skill.

There have been hospital studies comparing post-operative patients who were matched to screen out intervening variables. Some patients were in beds with a window view of green landscape, trees and sky. Others were in beds with no view of anything but the television set. The patients with window views tended to need less pain killers and evidenced quicker recoveries.

This is not difficult to believe. I have heard many stressed clients and friends refer to the peace and calm of sitting on their own patio, or the enormous satisfaction of laboring to build a backyard pond. Sometimes it is not just a scientific phenomenon, it is also a spiritual experience.

Frequently, I have seen this in my practice. People who have experienced isolation and pain in their lives become "grounded" in a more spiritual sense and gradually experience a sense of inner peace, which helps them to move beyond the feelings of isolation.

Sarah, a very kind and sensitive woman, with whom I worked for many, many hours, struggled with the aftermath of a painful and abusive childhood and an unhappy present. Her only pleasant memories were of the escape to the sanctuary of a woodland area near her home.

Then, in midlife, Sarah made a truly life-affirming decision. She moved to a new home in the country. Once again, she became a nurturer of woods and earth, and animals. The nurturer, herself, was nurtured. As the months went by, the healing would be visible to all who knew her. Sarah, herself, had begun to bloom.

Witnessing the healing quality of nature has been a recurring theme in my own life. Sometimes it has been an experience I have just stumbled upon. That was what happened a number of years ago when I directed the Listening Post, a YMCA-sponsored hotline and youth services center, which operated out of an apartment building across the street from a busy mall.

Many of the Listening Post youth were just normal, delightful teenagers going through the difficult times of adolescence. Some were emotionally disturbed, heavily drug involved, and busy abusing their minds and bodies. There was little room in their lives for social interactions or contact with the world of nature.

Wouldn't it be great, I fantasized, to create an alternative program for some of these youth, who now needed partial hospitalization just to function. After my own years of movement and physical training with the YMCA, I wanted to see the kids return to a sense of their physical self. Then maybe they could recapture that childhood ability to create one's own turn-on — to fly without chemical assistance.

That marked the birth of the "Body Shop" dream. At the time it did not seem too significant that my fitness training was not extensive, my dance background was limited, and my yoga expertise was minimal. Someone in the YMCA with more experience could direct this part of the project.

Not.

No one in the YMCA had the combined requirements of skills, interest in the project, and availability. So, if the Body Shop was going to fly, I was it. Fortunately, Steffi, my assistant director at the Listening Post, also had two out of three.

Well, why not, I decided. I might not have the skills to teach technique, but what I did have to offer was the feeling of body and dance that is present in all of us, to some degree. In this sense, there is no criteria for "quality" of performance. I could share that feeling, and help others to experience it. There. That is what I had to offer.

The Body Shop did not attempt to be some grandiose therapeutic substitute, just a very pleasant experience that could provide, for some, a whole new place to be. For others it would just be a simple, pleasing physical experience.

In addition to the benefit of the experience, one of the goals of the project was to provide an outlet for adolescent patients, many of whom the Listening Post referred to area mental health facilities. All too often, youth who are discharged from a psych unit then return to exactly the same destructive peer group environment which they left originally. The involvement with the Body Shop would give these youth an introduction to the Listening Post, and thus provide a place to which they could return for more positive social and group connections.

With this in mind, I volunteered my services to the psychiatric staff at a local hospital. The nursing staff was interested, but wary at first. I tried to convey to them verbally the concept that dance and body movement should be a source of spontaneity and pleasure for the untrained as well as the trained. This is possible for anyone once the feeling of awkwardness and self-consciousness are overcome.

Most of the nursing staff became enthusiastic supporters. On several occasions a nurse would comment that a particular patient had gotten a lot from the experience. That, I believe, has something to do with the fact that being aware of one's body and in tune with it can be the beginning of feeling good about one's self. In the beginning sessions of the Body Shop

I found that people liked to stretch and use their bodies in ways that were new to them. They felt most comfortable doing something that was different but still easy to do.

Throughout the sessions I continued to re-emphasize the fact that in this group there was no criteria for "performance." We were together just to share an experience that would be different for each of us just as each of our bodies was different. The criteria for "success" was how you felt doing something, not how you looked.

In the Body Shop we used a lot of yoga movement, which I had to preface with the clarification that I most definitely was not a yoga teacher. No one cared.

"A man is as young as his spine," says the yogis. "As you stretch and loosen your back your inner self will stretch and loosen." This may be a little exaggeration. I have known some self-proclaimed yogis who would certainly qualify as anal retentive. But basically, I agree. Rigidity begins when a person is not willing to change his attitude or his body. That can start in adolescence.

Doing yoga in a group is built around learning to attain various poses, or "postures." By assuming these positions the body is toned, builds flexibility and fluidity of movement, improves bodily functions and, perhaps most important, learns a kind of control.

As we learn control over our bodies we can also begin to learn to control our emotions. In learning this kind of control the student of yoga can begin to develop detachment; not from life, but from the pressures and fears that can make living difficult. It is just this quiet focus and concentration that can connect us to our own inner peace.

Learning these skills in the Body Shop utilized some of the same principles as the simpler behaviorist relaxation and desensitization methods. However, in addition to the same benefits the behaviorists claim, with yoga you can also build a stronger, healthier body.

On particularly warm and beautiful days we held the Body Shop outside and used the large expanse of lawn behind the hospital.

One morning as we started out, taking the elevator down from the sixth floor psychiatric unit, the elevator was stopped on a lower floor. But the lady who had pressed the button, upon seeing a number of us filling up the car, hesitated, and then stepped back to wait for the next car.

The momentary silence in the car was broken when Dorothy, who had already started the day in a bad mood, angrily pointed out that the lady probably just did not want to ride in the same car with the "crazies from the sixth floor." Dorothy was probably right and everyone knew it. That hurt.

"If it really bothers you," I suggested, "the next time you could carry a clipboard and act like you are one of the staff, and the rest of us are the patients." Everyone liked that suggestion, except the one staff member in the car.

Trivial as it might seem to an outsider, that experience was hurtful enough to make some of the patients feel uncomfortable as we trooped out through the lobby to head for the large, grassy back lawn behind the hospital. However, once outside, the beautiful weather and the feeling of just being free revived everyone's spirits.

Using a tape of "Zorba the Greek" on my loud portable cassette player, I suggested that we all make a chain and do a Greek dance across the lawn. Actually I don't even know how to Greek dance. I just made up a step I had seen on television, and we all put our arms around each other's shoulders and danced and danced around the yard until people started dropping off to lay on the grass, laughing and relaxing and feeling that innate connection with all aspects of the natural world.

In that moment, laughing and exhausted, there were no more "sixth floor crazies," no more staff and volunteers. Just people, together, forgetting stress and pain for awhile, and *being* the dance.

This is what happens in therapy. This is what happens in life and it is not new. It has been always; as in the old Hasidic saying:

> *I get up — I walk — I struggle —*
> *I fall down — I get up — I walk —*
> *I struggle — I stumble — I fall down —*
> *I get up — I keep dancing.*

And so it is for us all.

Poor, angry Dorothy, who was still feeling annoyed, was not quite willing to let it go.

"You don't even know how to do a Greek dance right," she snapped.

"I know," I admitted, "but wasn't it fun?" Dorothy thought about it for awhile, sniffed, and then, reluctantly, agreed.

Dancing well isn't important. Dancing is.

After everyone had stretched out on the soft grass and enjoyed the warm sun, no one wanted to return to the unit. Neither did I! We were all in such high spirits it just did not make sense to go back to the original program I had prepared. Instead, I suggested, wouldn't it be fun to roll down the steep grassy hill behind the hospital?

Steffi and I ran to the top of the hill and rolled down, whooping and hollering the entire way—which is the only proper way to roll down a hill. Before we reached the bottom a few others joined us. Soon most of the group were laughing and shouting and rolling down the hill.

"That was wonderful!" Dorothy gasped through her laughter, as we all sprawled on the ground trying to catch our breath. "I haven't had that much fun since I was a little girl."

And that was the first time I had ever seen Dorothy laugh.

Periodically, I had to remind the hospital staff that the Body shop was not a mandatory experience. They continued to pressure any patient who was "loitering around" into instant participation. That, I continued to point out, did tend to rob the process of any spontaneity. My support of "creative loitering" continued to be a losing battle. I just wanted people to feel free to be with us on whatever basis they chose to be there. On some occasions this could mean there were as many observers as there were participants.

However, when it was time for relaxation everyone participated. For the observers, just reveling in a green and calm world was a peaceful and relaxing experience. Just say the magic word "relaxation" at the Body Shop and dead silence fell as everyone stretched out, shut their eyes, and went limp.

It was not always like that. In the beginning session when we used relaxation, there were a few distractions that I did not learn about in my group counseling courses.

To begin with, it has been a bad day in "group" for everyone. "Group" being group therapy sessions held just prior to the Body Shop hour. I could always tell what had happened in the group by the first few minutes of Body Shop. Today it had been bad. Everyone was still "acting out," as the staff nurse kept remarking pointedly.

Maureen, who at 35 weighed in at 260 pounds of pure misery, was loud and surly. Life had not been kind to Maureen in her early years. Under the anger and shouting was an unhappy, empty, little girl, who wanted only to be filled. But she didn't know how. And all the cookies in the world couldn't do it. Maureen had spent the first portion of the class greeting everyone near her with the admonition, "Don't touch me!" All during the exercise session she kept a bulging cloth bag by her side.

"Don't touch my things," she warned whenever anyone came too close to the cloth bag.

Jean sat over in the corner by herself with her back to the group.

And Gail announced that she could "do these stupid exercises better than anyone else."

"Sh-h-h," sniffed Helen, "no one wants to hear you anyway."

"Just settle back and close your eyes . . . .," I continued quietly, going ahead with the relaxation session.

Crackle, crackle, crackle . . . went the wrapper from the cookie package Maureen had hidden in her cloth bag.

"Maureen, we are *all* doing this together," broke in the firm voice of the nurse who had joined us. "You can't eat and be part of this group at the same time."

Kathy snickered loudly.

"You all hate me," whimpered Maureen.

Someone muttered something, and Kathy snickered again. This time the nurse interceded. I waited until she had finished and then suggested quietly to her that I would like to carry it alone from here. Slowly, the group worked back to the beginning of a relaxation session.

"... take a deep breath and let it out slowly. Feel how heavy and relaxed you have become ..."

A slight whisper from Maureen broke the silence.

"Shut your goddamn mouth!" bellowed Gail. "I am relaxing."

Maureen whimpered again and reached for her cookies.

"If you can't cooperate," broke in the nurse, "you'll have to go back on the ward. You're not going to stay here and spoil it for everyone. . . "

"Shut your goddamn mouth," repeated Gail.

Barbara stood up, calmly took off her blouse and walked away. I left the nurse to worry about Barbara, which solved two problems, while I walked over to Maureen. Sitting down very close to her I put my hand on her arm and began talking very quietly. Gradually, I let my voice raise just enough for the others to hear me if they were very quiet.

"You've had a very rough morning, I guess." I smiled at Maureen. "It must be really hard to just let go and relax. Maybe I could do it with you while I talk, and then everyone else could just sort of follow us."

And so we started once more. But this time as I said "Just settle back and relax and enjoy the feeling of pleasantness. . . , " Maureen did begin to relax and let go. Others began to get in touch with the feeling, too.

Afterwards we talked about the afternoon and how each person had experienced it. That was the beginning of something really powerful between us all. In a way, that was the day we became a group.

Two weeks later, on another glorious day, we dumped our plans for an organized class indoors and went for a walk down a wooded path behind the hospital grounds. At first we began as a trust walk, joining hands and walking very slowly single file down the path.

Steffi and myself were on either end of the line. It became an experience of real sensitivity to the environment, feeling anew the wind on our faces, the roughness of the ground underfoot, the thick bark of the trees, and most of all, the sunshine on our heads.

Afterwards, we walked back together talking and laughing in little groups. Steffi walked along with Susan and Lisa, both in their late teens. These were the two who for weeks had been so angry with each other they had barely spoken. Now they had become close friends and confidants. It was a delight to see them laughing and acting like the teenagers they were.

Lisa was bubbling with pleasure because she was to be discharged from the program that afternoon.

"That's great, Lisa," said Susan in a flat voice that combined pleasure for her friend with a tinge of envy for herself. "Now you have a whole life ahead of you."

"So do you, Susan," said Lisa, suddenly serious, "if you want it."

"I wish I wanted it," mumbled Susan.

"I'm going to get you out of this mood if it kills me," said Lisa, almost angry now. Susan looked bewildered, uncertain now whether to be pleased, or hurt, or angry.

"I think she's saying that she really cares about you, Susan," interjected Steffi.

"I do," said Lisa, smiling shyly and then looking quickly at a point to the left of Susan's shoulder.

"I like her, too," smiled Susan, looking down at her shoes.

"Well, that's what it's all about," said Steffi, who was still earnest enough to get away with remarks like that.

It was through experiences like these over the months that a lot of trust built up within the Body Shop group. And even as the original group slowly changed, losing some old members and adding some new ones, the feeling was passed on.

One of the best examples of this came one morning at the Body Shop after a period of deep relaxation on a grassy slope, followed by the group learning to do face massages on each other. Afterwards. we had spontaneous and very deep discussion about intimacy, and the desire for, and sometimes fear of, touching.

Ellen, a gentle, tired looking woman in her forties, had not wanted to participate at first. A victim of both parental and spousal abuse, Ellen had been struck in the face numerous times, and maintained fearfully, "I *hate* being touched, *ever*." After sharing in the relaxation part of the Body Shop, Ellen very gingerly responded to my invitation to try the experience of face massage.

First we talked briefly about the sadness of knowing that the years of abuse had not only inflicted intense pain, but also had robbed Ellen of the pleasure of experiencing a caring touch.

"It's okay," I soothed her fears, "I'll be the one to work with you. If at any point you're feeling anxious, we can just switch positions without any discomfort for you."

Ellen thought about it for a long time. I could see by her face that she was struggling between feelings of desire for a pleasant experience and the feeling of fear.

"Wouldn't it be lovely," I suggested, "to find a whole new pleasant experience you've never had before?"

Trust won. With great hesitation Ellen joined us. I treated her with all the tenderness and gentleness I could, as I demonstrated to the class how to make a face massage a deeply pleasurable experience for someone else. Gradually Ellen let herself relax and slip into the experience. It was a delight to watch her face as it first relaxed and then eased into pure pleasure.

The next time around it was Ellen who, with great gentleness, provided the face massage for someone else. It was a powerful moment to see Ellen start to trust and to feel good about her own body and most of all about herself, and then to watch her show that, in a caring, touching act for someone else.

Dancing well isn't important. Dancing is.

CHAPTER 9

# *A Time*
# *to Laugh*

*And why do you worry about clothing?*
*Consider the lilies of the field, how they grow;*
*they neither toil nor spin . . . But if God*
*so clothes the grass of the field, which is*
*alive today and tomorrow is thrown into*
*the oven, will He not much more clothe you?*
—Matthew 6:28-30

he lilies of the field speak to the celebration of the glory of the earth. A reminder to every gardener that toil in the garden is not an end in itself. It is only a preface to the celebration of the divine in the garden.

So, as spring rolls into summer, I prepare for less toil and more celebration. It is time to roll back into my garden uniform: old jeans, old t-shirt, old sneakers, and, of course, my old dolphin garden hat.

The hat, all floppy, frayed-out denim, is liberally dosed with herbal bug repellent. Most of the time it keeps both the sun and the bugs off my face. Even if it performed neither of these functions, I would wear it anyway. This is the talisman of sunny days in the Bahamas. The highlight of those days being the return visits to the dolphins of the Blue Lagoon Island.

Second only to my wedding portraits and photographs of my family, are the laughing shots of Stan and myself on the sloppy end of a dolphin kiss. If you have never hugged one of these gentle creatures, it is an experience not to be missed. God really outdid Himself when he created the dolphin. It kind of makes up for His goof with the slugs.

I spotted this hat while riding the return ferryboat from the Blue Lagoon. It was a lovely shade of faded blue denim with the "Dolphin Encounters" logo embroidered in yellow on the crown. As someone who rarely goes in tourist shops or buys souvenirs, I was surprised by how badly I wanted this one.

There was one small complication. This hat was resting on the head of the ferryboat captain. Well, boldness can sometimes be a virtue, I reassured myself. Joining the captain at the wheel, I came straight to the point.

"Would you like to sell your hat?"

"I'm not allowed to take it off," he laughed.

"Why not?" I wondered out loud. In response the captain pulled off his hat and out popped the most magnificent afro I have ever seen. It was thick, luxuriant, and took up more space than I could imagine was in that hat.

"The management doesn't want staff members to have big hair," he explained. "The tourists might not like it." We both concurred that the tourists should just worry about their own hair.

"What about borrowing a hat for the ride back, and selling me this one for $20?" I suggested. Knowing that as a staff member he could get another one free, the captain decided that this would be a reasonable deal. The hat was shifted quickly into my swimming suit bag, and $20 was stuffed quickly into his hand. A casual observer might well have wondered what transaction had just taken place.

Stan later questioned the wisdom of this deal. For, when we returned to our stateroom and dumped out our swimming suit bags, we were nearly overcome by the stench that arose. It smelled like a dead animal that has been sprayed with cheap perfume. Three washings in the stateroom sink failed to completely remove the lingering odor. We finally concluded that the captain must have used large amounts of conditioning lotion, or hair gel that turned rancid in the heat.

Finally, I sealed the offending hat in two plastic bags for the return home. Upon arriving home, the poor hat was repeatedly washed and bleached into a remnant of its former glory. But it is my hat and I like it.

But, more important than hats, or working in the garden, it is sum-

mer, it is time to just "be" in the garden. It is time for family, friends and laughter. It is time for the movable feast.

In our garden that means, don't just walk straight through. Stop at a bench or a table just to enjoy where you are. And, as A.A Milne's "Winnie the Pooh" is so fond of saying: "have a little something." With this is mind, the garden is filled with little rest stops. Places where you can, as the hymn says: "Come and find the quiet center . . . be at peace and simply be."

Stone benches are tucked along the edges of the paths. The pergola would not be complete without its log chairs and table. In the wooded area two teak benches flank a low deacon's table, and the gazebo is filled with adirondack chairs, surrounding a round, wooden table. They are all just waiting for passersby to pause for a snack, or just to sit with a steaming cup of coffee.

Each table area can, at a moment's notice, be ready to be covered with a checked tablecloth, and topped with whatever potted flower is currently blooming. This is where Michelle, my granddaughter, has been known to enjoy an occasional teddy bear tea party. With lots of sugar, please.

Brian and Patrick, my grandsons, prefer the long, L-shaped picnic table on the patio. For family get-togethers the table is often set with pewter plates, which look wonderful and are virtually indestructible; and with a series of flower filled old crocks. The antique, one-handled, white crockery chamber pots from England are charming when filled with ferns or geraniums.

It does make you wonder, though. The chamber pots are not that big, just about the size of a small soup tureen. What would have happened if the user of the chamber pot had awakened in the middle of the night after having had too much to drink the night before? It made Stan wonder, too. He has been heard warning buffet guests to avoid any one-handled soup tureens.

I have always suspected that the real reason the boys preferred to dine at the patio picnic table was due, in large part, to the collection of soleri bells which hang from the arbor above the table. It is amazing that the bells have survived the boys' earlier years, for they suffered many hours of ruthless pulling, twisting, and loud, competitive clanging.

All this mealtime chaos would have been difficult for my mother, who preferred a more quiet "genteel" meal, with crystal and china and soft voices. The presentation was always lovely, but the content usually left a little to be desired. This was due, in part, to the fact that Mother liked to cook and steam everything until it was all the same color: a soft, brown-ish gray earth tone.

Cooking-wise, I am my mother's daughter, which is probably why we both became sugar fanatics. For us, there was no meal or food item that could not be vastly improved by the addition of sugar. Until recently, when my body started protesting, my idea of the perfect breakfast was Hershey bars and coffee. Fortunately, for me, the women in my family do not get fat. They just become increasingly fluffy. It took me a long time to come to the realization that Hershey bars and coffee are good for a "buzz," but bad for "fluffy."

The worst Hershey bar days did not occur until after my children were grown. When Tara and Kevin were young I earnestly tried to be "Ms Better Homes and Gardens," so they would grow up to be well nourished and at home in the kitchen. Quite possibly, I have overrated my success in this area.

Recently, I told John, my son-in-law, that I had taught Tara everything I know about cooking

"That probably took about 15 minutes," he said, after he stopped laughing.

Easy for him to say. He is an excellent cook. Well, lucky us. Both of our children were clever enough to marry good cooks. And what is even more important, they picked partners that we also loved.

Sometimes I wonder at my good fortune to have been blessed with my own two wonderful children, and then to have both John, and Pacita, my beautiful daughter-in-law, who has called me "Mom" for so long I sometimes forget that she wasn't born to me. Seeing my two daughters joining in laughter, heads together; one dark and shiny, the other blonde and fluffy; I know that I am truly blessed.

Best of all in the summer, is the time for family festivals. In our family a festival is just a time for the extended family and friends to spend a day together in the garden, laughing and playing and eating.

Any reason for a festival will suffice. In the past we have had the "Great Petunia Festival," the Great Croquet Tournament," and the "Great Art Festival". For the latter, an impressionist artist from Arkansas drove to Maryland in a van loaded with oil paintings, which were then hung around the patio, in the gazebo and on the trees. He also invited a whole entourage of local artists. That was fun. The festivals are all fun. That is why they are always preceded by the word "great."

When the extended family, which includes the children and grandchildren of my brother, gathers for a festival, it is always chaotic, noisy and fun. Although we are not morning people, on festival days Stan and I are always up early. There are chairs and tables and bricks to be hosed off, as well as children's projects to be planned, and food platters to be prepared.

The garden of solitude will soon be a garden of people and activity and noise, lots of noise. But, first, in the early hours, there is my quiet time. The garden is hushed and waiting. I retreat to the hammock and watch the morning unfold around me. The air is fresh, and it smells warm and damp and clean. I love the thought of experiencing this quiet beauty every morning, but, I just don't love the idea of getting up so early to do it. Maybe someday.

Soon the birds are conversing with each other, and the squirrels have begun racing about on the tree branches. It is time to get in gear.

The first step before the chores begin is to prepare the trash area for today's onslaught. Trash bags need to be laid out and extra recycle bins at the ready. All too often, I discover that Wilma, the raccoon, has preceded me. The trash area is now littered with the remains of her nightly meal, plus whatever items she removed from the garbage can, but did not find sufficiently attractive to consume.

Good environmentalist that I am, I would like to put my hands around her neck. But by now, Wilma has long since returned to her dark corner under the deck. She thinks that I don't know she's there. But, I do.

Sometimes, as I do my pre-festival check of every corner of the garden, I come across Fred, the turtle. Fred was a gift from Lisa, our neighbor, who, before she morphed into a beautiful teenager, liked to collect animals. When Fred arrived at his new garden, Lisa and I spent consider-

able time making a charming little home for him, complete with food and water and high stone walls. We thought it was charming. Fred thought it stunk.

Fred was right. He knew a cage when he saw one. Within 24 hours Fred was history. Since then, he just shows up when he feels like it, which is seldom. Sometimes, when I spot Fred before a festival I consider putting him in a box for the children to see. But no, better to discard that idea. It wouldn't be fair to him. This is his day, too. And Fred hates the children.

By early afternoon people begin to arrive. Food offerings appear. This is good. We will not have to depend on my deli offerings. The tub of soft drinks is iced. Soon there is the clanging of the soleri bells. Solitude has been replaced by laughter. It is going to be a good day. And I am filled with gratitude.

Now the garden tours can begin. Although I am delighted to show every wonderful thing in the garden to all present, I have reluctantly come to realize that these tours are not of universal interest to everyone. Usually, it is the children who will accompany me.

After many tours a ritual has emerged. As Patrick is always reminding us, "it's a tradition." The tour must always start at the peace arch and wind through the meditation garden. By now, we have lost at least one person, usually a derelict boy, who simply has to toss a few stones in the pond. This practice is about to be eliminated from the "tradition" list, for there is now a family of tadpoles to be considered.

As the garden tour winds through the meditation garden, and down the needle path to the entry arch at the children's park, the girls become more interested. This is because here is where the statues begin.

Each girl cousin is represented by a stone statue. The boys have declined this honor. Even in kindergarten and elementary school, boys are not about to be identified as angels, sprites, and cherubs.

The statue "tradition" started quite by accident. One day, while browsing at a local nursery, I was enchanted by a weathered stone statue of a young Victorian girl. Her sweet, little face with the shy smile bore an uncanny resemblance to our little grandniece, Amy. She was irresistible. So home she came to the children's park.

Amy was soon joined by her sister, Chrissy, who appeared as a bright, saucy cherub. She now sits on a flat rock, hands clasped around her knees, gazing impishly at any passing observers.

Well, needless to say, when there are seven little girls, it is quite necessary that there be seven little statues.

Shaded by the woodland nandina bush, stands Michelle, our angel. Looking every bit the part, she holds a small dove, and stands tall among the ferns. The reason she is standing tall, says Michelle, is because *she* is the granddaughter, and as such, she should have the biggest statue.

Margaret, her cousin, is represented by the statue of a beautiful young woman, seated on an oval rock inside the stone basin at the entry to the children's park. She is poised and serene, a mirror of the young woman her namesake will one day become.

Around the corner, a light stone birdbath is topped with a small graceful sprite, kneeling in the water. This would have to be Olivia, the slender, lithe dancer.

"She really looks like you," I told Olivia.

"Yes," replied Olivia, shyly, hesitating. "But," she added plaintively, "I wish she had on some clothes."

"Where's my statue, Allie?" questioned four-year old Emily. "Everyone has a statue but me."

"But, you have the ladybug," I pointed out. The ladybug is a low, carved, oval table on iron legs, that I had painted to look like a ladybug. Quite well, I might add. Many pictures had been taken of a younger Emily astride the ladybug.

"But, Allie," she protested, "a ladybug is not person."

"Well, then, I guess we'll just have to find a statue that looks like Emily." I agreed. Now where in the garden, I wondered, was there a statue of a bouncy, curly-headed little girl?

Taking my hand, Emily walked all through the garden, searching for her replica.

"Here she is! Here she is!" cried Emily, stopping suddenly by the lovely, tranquil, and quite womanly looking angel that knelt in the ferns at the end of the hammock.

"Oh," breathed Emily, "she looks just like me." We had found Emily's statue.

"Me! Me!" echoed Megan, the toddler. She may have been the youngest, but Megan was no "tail-end Charlie." Bright and quick, Megan was always front and center.

She soon found her look-alike in a small, smiling cherub that nestled beneath the Pieris Japonica at the end of the path.

And now, no more babies. We have run out of statues.

The garden tour leads straight to the Children's Park. It was Patrick, who at age five, dreamed up the idea for the "park." It was one of those lazy summer days when he decided to come over and help with the gardening chores. These "help" sessions usually entailed about five minutes of weeding and two hours of playing games.

Most of the games involved adventures with Patrick as the hero, and Allie as the straight man. Sometimes, he was "Ole, The Wonder Man," and I was "Queen Baba-Lu." Then there were the horses. To the uninitiated, they might have appeared just to be sawhorses to which necks and heads had been added. But we knew better. Of course, Patrick always got "Thunder, the Magic Horse," and I always got "Thor, The Wicked Horse."

The children's park idea was hatched as Patrick was cleaning brush and debris from the neglected back section of the garden. While picking up sticks, Patrick pointed out that there was more garden space than there was play space, so this area should become a children's park. Well, why not?

When he realized that his idea was to become a reality, Patrick spent the remainder of the afternoon clearing with a passion. Every scrap of debris had to go.

Plans were made for what he dubbed, "the chatting corner." This included a semi-circle of wooden chairs around a huge, old stump "table."

The red sawhorses now made their home in the park, and a hammock — "just for kids" — was hung between two large pine trees. A "beach" was formed with the addition of many wheelbarrow loads of river jack, the round, smooth, potato-sized rocks which curved around the left perimeter of the park.

Not to be outdone, Brian, the craftsman, created his own masterpiece for the Children's Park; an elaborate set of wind chimes composed of ice cream carton lids and sea shells. As the artist, Brian reserved the right to select the correct and most prominent placement for the chimes.

"If people ask you who made this," Brian earnestly assured me, "it would be okay to use my name."

Using carpenter's scraps for my contribution, I was able to create a large supply of building blocks, which were carefully sanded and painted. These blocks become the buildings and roadways for the boys' many wars and matchbox car races. So, while it was always Stan who took the boys on their weekend "guy" excursions, I was the one in the children's park learning to make boy noises, complete with racing car engines, squealing brakes, and massive traffic pile-ups.

On festival days, the children's park hammock bears the brunt of many kids, all using the hammock at the same time. It is understood by all, that the adults' hammock, nestled in the woodland area, and surrounded by ferns, is for stodgy, old people. These are people who tend to use the hammock one at a time, and are not inclined to turn it upside down.

During one recent festival, I got particularly grumpy with Brian for joining with his cousins to use the adult hammock like a carnival ride, and mashing several ferns in the process. No one in this family suffers in silence, and that day I was no exception.

Still protesting his innocence, Brian quickly departed in search of better company, which he found soon enough. Following the shouts of laughter, I entered the children's park in time to see Brian swinging his cousins, Max and James, in a hammock that was about to go airborne.

"Uh, oh," I overheard Brian gasp between laughs, "I forgot, I have to be careful, or Allie won't let me back in the garden until I have a beard."

No matter where the garden tour starts, the destination is always the swimming pool, which has been the center of many, happy festival days. When the pool went in, we were warned by several friends that a swimming pool is just a big hole in the ground into which you throw a lot of money. This is true. But, oh, the sparkle on the water, and the clean, cool feeling when you slide in. Delicious.

All the sweeter for me, for I still remember the summer I was ten and dreamed of having a family pool of our own. However, my father had his own ideas about dealing with impractical dreams.

"Too expensive," he said. "But, if you can dig a swimming pool then you can have one."

That became the summer of the great dig. Every day I went to the designated pool site, in the far corner of the back yard, and dug and dug and dug. It was hot, dirty work, but whenever I got tired I would imagine the crystal clear blue water that would soon be right in this spot. By late summer I had succeeded in creating a hole nearly the size of two bathtubs.

One day, with no warning, reality struck. Tired and sweaty, I leaned on my shovel and gazed up at the house. There, staring from the living room window, was my father's face. He was watching me, and he was laughing. In that moment I knew that there would never be a pool.

For several years the hole remained. Every rainy season it filled with water, which slowly drained, leaving behind a great bowl of muck. Every time I saw that hole I made a vow. Someday, I promised myself, there will be a pool. Now there is.

Our festival pool is a bit bigger than the dream pool of my childhood, but it is by no means large. A long, narrow lap pool, it is close to overflowing if all eleven children and assorted aunts and uncles are present. There are also other important details to be considered. There are eleven children. There must be eleven plastic inner tubes. They must be different colors. There must be enough non-pink tubes to insure that no boy will have to suffer the humiliation of using a pink tube.

The gazebo overlooks the pool. This is the adult hang-out. Everyone concurs with the unbreakable rule that at all times there must be at least four adults in the gazebo to watch the swimmers. This has never been a problem. The drinks are also in the gazebo.

Some of the special moments of festival days are those spent in the gazebo with family and friends, laughing and talking; and watching the kids, laughing and shouting.

"Hey, look at me!"

"Watch this! Watch this!"

"No! No! Don't splash me!"

"Quick! Somebody take a picture of this!"

Gradually, the shrieking and the sounds of carousing die down, and one by one, the kids come to the gazebo to just sit and talk with family. There is an easy comfort, with adults and children just enjoying the company of each other. These are the magic moments, when you see anew the special, sweet quality of each child.

The children do not yet recognize what a treasured moment they have given a parent, or grandparent, at these times when they reach out with a little kindness of their own. Like Michelle, who shyly hands me a note:

At the close of a long festival day everyone is feeling mellow and well fed. It is time for hugs and goodbyes, and let's do it again soon. The children, too, are sensitive to the poignancy of this moment.

One of my fond memories is of Brian and Patrick, tired and happy, at the close of a long, full day. Seated together on top of the patio railing, they stared up at the stars, oblivious to everyone else.

"Don't you just love coming to Allie and Poppy's," whispered Patrick.

"Yes," echoed Brian, "I just want to re-wind this whole day and run it all over again."

And so do I.

CHAPTER 10

# A Time
# to Lose

*Life is short and we do not
have too much time to gladden
the hearts of those who
travel with us, so be swift
to love and make haste
to be kind.*
—Henri-Frédéric Amiel

When the festival is over and the last child has left, the garden, once again, is quiet. The stillness is broken only by the splash of the pond. It is time to sit back and savor the day.

Sitting quietly in the weather-beaten, wooden adirondack chair that I had once bought for my dear friend, Alta, I remember again all her joyous laughter when, she too, was a part of the festival.

Some of our happiest moments together were spent walking along the paths, talking and laughing together. Ultimately, we would end up on a stone bench or seated on the edge of the herb bed, feeling at peace in the calm of the warm sun. These are the times when you know that the garden has truly become a gift to the spirit

My first memories of Alta were from when I was just a kid and she was a young government worker, living with relatives and struggling through law school. I used to visit her family with my parents. The only reason I tagged along was because I always hoped that Alta would be there. She was so vital and independent and full of fun — just the kind of woman I wanted to be.

Alta always found my pre-adolescent behavior amusing and often teased, "You'd better plan to marry early, honey, because you're never going to make it in a career."

"On second thought," she added fondly, "maybe you better have a career. You're too much of a dreamer to be a homemaker."

Let it be noted that it was not necessary that Alta always be right in order for her to render an opinion.

Our worlds were very different then. While I was growing up, Alta finished law school and went on to a career in the Justice Department. After many years of law practice, Alta met the love of her life, Joe. Soon a wedding was planned.

Naturally, Alta, the gourmet cook, was given a bridal shower by her close friends and fellow gourmets. Each guest, as directed by the invitation, brought what she considered to be the ultimate gift — a little 3 x 5 file card imprinted with the directions for her most treasured recipe.

I was probably invited to the shower as a courtesy to the family, for, as a new bride, my culinary skills were on a par with Ronald McDonald. My contribution to the recipe book was a three-line recipe for succotash. Essentially, this recipe called for mixing one bag of frozen corn with one bag of lima beans.

Alta accepted my contribution with all the dignity and grace she had accorded the others. But, in later years, she never let me forget it. And we laughed a lot about that.

It was a number of years later before I returned to the area. One of the wonderful gifts I got from joining my church was the arrival of Alta, who soon became a special part of the church community, and of my life.

In the years that passed, Alta gave so much to so many people. When an old friend was in deep legal trouble in another state, Alta was there to provide legal assistance. She didn't look very fierce with her gentle face, and barely 115 pounds on a 5'4" frame. But, Alta became the great pit bull of justice in those weeks. The opposition was pulverized. Alta never let go until her friend's life was once again in order.

It was that same kind of fierce caring that Alta also brought, even to people she did not know well. Although she was always getting involved in Christian mission projects, it was the little connections she made along the way; the seeing that someone was hurting and caring enough to stop and listen, that really spoke to who she was.

Although deeply religious, Alta never lost her delightful touch of irreverence. She had a tongue like a rapier. And this, too, was part of her charm. I enjoyed her far more than I would have enjoyed someone closer to sainthood.

She gave so much to the church, to others and to me. All this, even though she once did sit at a church dinner where the subject of my earlier book, "The God Squad," was discussed.

"I knew Alice when she was just a little thing," Alta loudly announced to the entire table, in her own inimitable Kentucky twang. "I never did think she would amount to a hill of beans." I never let her forget that. And it made us laugh a lot.

By this time I was deep in the garden, and the festivals had begun. As always, the festivals were just an excuse for family and friends to get together and laugh and celebrate life. Alta was always there, and we always laughed, a lot.

Sometimes I laughed too much and forgot the food burning on the stove. But Alta never did. At first she would nudge me and mention that the burning smell might have some significance. Soon she would just rescue it herself. Ultimately, she just took over the food preparation. Fondly, I would call her "Martha in the Kitchen."

The "Martha" title was our ongoing joke. Martha and Mary, in the Bible story, are sisters who have welcomed Jesus into their home. During His visit Mary sits at Jesus' feet and listens raptly to His teachings, while Martha labors alone to prepare a meal. Increasingly irritated that she is doing all the work while Mary gets to enjoy Jesus, Martha stomps out of the kitchen and joins them.

"Lord, do you not care that my sister has left me to serve alone? Tell her then to help me."

"Martha, Martha," chides Jesus. "You are anxious and troubled about

many things; one thing is needful. Mary has chosen the good portion, which shall not be taken away from her." Luke 10:38-42

I am probably more like Mary than Martha. Nonetheless, I have always thought that poor Martha got a bum rap. Historically, she has often been portrayed as the non-spiritual, whining complainer, who has missed the whole point of Jesus' coming. But, what if you look at Martha as the provider of food and sustenance; the one who feeds and clothes and nurtures, so others may be able to experience life more fully?

There are lots of useless "spiritual" people in the world who sit on mountain tops and talk only about *their* quest for God. But they never hear the call of God to feed the hungry and clothe the poor. And while these "searchers" remain on their mountain tops ruminating about "God and me," or maybe just "Me and god," it is often the Marthas who are feeding the hungry and clothing the poor.

I like to think that while Jesus was chiding Martha, He was also opening His arms to offer her a place at the table.

Alta was one of those special "Marthas" who make cooking an art and a gift. We used to joke that dinner at Alta's house was a feast, both beautiful and nurturing. While dinners at my house were always carry-out; or else partially prepared by Alta. That didn't matter to Alta because we always laughed a lot.

Sometimes we met at McDonald's. This was a place you would expect to find me, but not Alta, the gourmet. She would pop in after one of her long walks and discover that that was just the time when I would be having my midday feeding frenzy.

"God set that up," Alta insisted. "He just meant for us to talk." That was fine with me, I replied. But God might have picked some place a bit more upscale.

We would sit in those vinyl booths, drinking cups of that terrible coffee, and talk and talk. Sometimes we would talk about sadness or painful issues, the parts of life we all share. But not for too long, because Alta would always have to add, "and tell me, how are the kids?" And, of course, we laughed a lot.

That laughter was always one of the ways Alta and I experienced a deep closeness in our relationship. And that is what I believe we are meant to do in this world; laugh a lot.

Not all clergy share this view. "Preach," my Methodist pastor during my early college years, was a gentle, caring man, but not noticeably funny. I belatedly came to this conclusion after repeating several anecdotes that apparently were amusing only to me. At least, I was the only one laughing.

"Alice," Preach asked perplexedly, "do you think that God has a sense of humor?"

"Oh, yes."

"Well," he replied dubiously, "for your sake I hope he does."

I'm not worried.

Then suddenly everything changed. Alta was diagnosed with bone cancer, which had metastasized from an earlier bout with breast cancer. While Alta was recuperating at home from a long and painful hospital stay, I was at home recovering from an accident, which had resulted in a shattered knee.

This was a time of loss. I knew that I would walk again, but I didn't know how well. I had already been informed that I would always have some level of disability. This can be more attractively presented as "a few limitations." Dancing, jumping and running would no longer be options.

Dancing?, I questioned. No way. I'll just learn not to take both feet off the floor at the same time.

"Oh, don't worry," one of my friends consoled me, "everyone knows white women can't dance anyway." Now that helped.

But, when I thought about Alta, struggling for her life, one little knee didn't seem like such a big deal.

We continued to call each other and exchange our many war stories over the phone. One thing was agreed: we were both among the lucky ones. For we had husbands who were always there, and who always cared. We were not going to be handicapped, we vowed. "Mobility challenged" was our theme. A covenant was made: whoever became mobile first would be the one to make the visit to the other one's house with a bottle of champagne.

When I graduated from a wheelchair to a walker, I was the one to

Rose

make the trip to Alta's house. But there was no bottle of champagne. It would not have mixed well with the chemo. Instead, it was Alta who filled me with chocolates. We laughed at ourselves in the walkers. "The lame and the halt . . . ," we joked. Could there be a message here?

I hated my walker and raged at it as if it were a cage. Alta was more graceful about it all. For her, those aluminum frames were just another step toward the goal of recovery. So she conned me into having our pictures taken together, hanging in our walkers with our arms around each other, laughing a lot.

"Be sure to save your walker," Alta reminded me. "I'm keeping mine. It always gets me to the front of the line in restaurants."

The following Easter Alta came to her last festival. I had bought special adirondack chairs so she could sit on the patio in comfort and safety, and still be joined by others. This meant buying several chairs, for, if there was only one comfortable chair, Alta would have insisted that someone else sit there.

As planned, Alta settled comfortably in her new chair, but not for long. Soon "Martha" was back in the kitchen giving orders. Once again, she was taking over and making everything work.

And once again, when "Martha" had completed her tasks, we were back to our quiet place in the garden. Just being together, like so many times before.

"What a relief," sighed Alta, "just to say the things I need to say, and not have someone tell me it's going to be alright."

We talked a lot that day, about life and death, and families and friends. Alta rejoiced in the caring and love she was receiving, and shared plans for a last visit from her daughter, who would be returning from Seattle to be with her mother. We cried a little. And later of course, we laughed a lot.

Now, as I sit on the patio in one of "Alta's chairs" I can still see her

sitting here talking and laughing and just "being there" for everyone else. And exuding what Dag Hammarskjold called "that steady radiance, of a wonder, the source of which is beyond all reason." I want to laugh with her just one more time. And to tell her, "Alta, you achieved what we all hope for. You left the world a little better place."

"And you laughed a lot."

CHAPTER 11

# *A Time to Pause*

*Biden or not biden*
*God is Present*

There are times in the garden, as in life, when you just need to pause along the path. For me, working in the garden is sometimes hard work, often sweaty, occasionally tiring; but always enriching. Even so, I need to be aware when it is time to chuck out the chores, and just "be" at one with the garden.

Taking the time to pause in the garden, and to be at one with the world around me, never fails to stir in me a sense of wonder and awe. Buddhists would call this the sacred pause, and would liken it to the experience of the Buddha, when he stopped "doing" and simply sat under the bodhi tree and opened himself to "being."

The bodhi tree, for me, is the prayer rock, a magnificent old stone at the edge of the pond in the meditation garden. "Magnificent," is not a word others might choose for this four foot long, two foot high, lumpy rock, whose proportions resemble nothing so much as a giant, gray, pock-marked chunk of cheddar cheese. But, if you love old, weathered stones, then you will see the strong beauty in this massive prayer rock with its soft earth tones dappled with the subtle green shadings of fuzzy lichen nestled in the stone creases.

On late summer afternoons I like to sit on the warm, old stone and watch the sunlight filtering through the hollies and sparkling onto the pond falls. Atop the falls there is a shallow basin formed by a small pondlet, which provides the water for the falls.

Here is where the birds congregate for baths and chatter. At first the birds thought that I was up to no good, and quickly scattered upon my arrival. Gradually, as I continued to remain quite still and silent, the birds returned. Now they realize that I, too, come in peace.

The prayer rock was never really planned. Like so many good things in life, it just sort of emerged. One summer afternoon after a heavy storm had downed a multitude of heavy tree limbs, the garden was trashed with branches too heavy for Stan and me to remove. Like Scarlett O'Hara, I decided to "think about it tomorrow." Time to go for a frappacino.

One frappacino later, I wandered through the shopping center parking lot, following the siren song of chain saws. Sure enough, there was a landscape crew clearing the felled branches at the edge of the parking lot.

"Want to do a real quickie job just down the road?" I asked the crew foreman. Negotiations were made and the crew followed me home. They made quick order of the debris and stopped to admire the remainder of the garden. Surrounded by hollies, ferns, and wildflowers and edged with rounded river stones, the pond was the star attraction.

"What a great place for a stone bench," we all agreed. Well, actually, I sort of pushed the idea. But they liked it. When I started mapping out dimensions, one of the crew remembered seeing a boulder about that size in the weeds at the back of the landscaper's property

After a couple phone calls to the boss with relayed measurements, complete with color and textural descriptions, I knew that this was to be my rock. So, why wait around and obsess about it?, is my motto. Just leap right in. We agreed that he would deliver it immediately, in good faith. And I, in good faith, would buy it sight unseen. After all, boulders are not the sort of thing one returns.

The minute the boulder arrived, dragged in chains by four tired, sweating men, I knew that I had made the right choice. The men, however, had already come to the conclusion that they had not made the right choice of employment.

Not only was this a powerfully heavy boulder, they also had to contend with dragging it along a twisted, circuitous path, and listen to a crazy lady walking backward in front of them, pleading at every turn: "Oh, please be careful of that azalea. Watch out for the little fern."

It only got worse when we arrived at the pond, which was angled in at the edge of the meditation garden. The placement of the rock had to be aligned so that it was on the same plane as the pond. Otherwise, the harmony and flow of the garden would be disrupted.

Try explaining that to a group of Hispanic workers when the only Spanish words you know are "si," "gracias," "mas," (left) and "gordo," (fat.). "Backward," "forward," and "right" were not in my vocabulary. Each time I gestured to the men to shift the position ever so slightly they would nod vigorously, "Si, Si," and proceed to plop the rock in the general direction I had indicated.

"Oh, no," I kept shaking my head. "Now it's too far back." Or else, it was too far forward, or too far to the right. Each time the men heaved a great collective sigh, and once more, grunting and struggling, maneuvered the boulder into yet another position.

At last, after much arm waving, head nodding and shaking, and some creative charades, we finally got it just right. It was more than right. It was perfect.

Exuberantly, I shouted, "Yes! Yes! Yes; Oops, I mean si!" Hopping around like a demented fox terrier, I continued to exclaim over the absolute perfection of the now completed meditation garden.

"Oh gracias, gracias," I thanked them profusely for their unfailing good nature. They understood that. And we all laughed.

The prayer rock had arrived. I didn't call it that at first. I just knew that I liked to sit in silence on that comforting stone and be at one with the earth. Here was a place I could sort things out. A place where I could feel and listen.

This is not a place for words. It is a place for the experience of comfort. Saint Paul said it a little better in his letter to the Romans: "Likewise the Spirit helps us in our weakness; for we do not know how to pray as we ought, but the spirit intercedes for us with sighs too deep for words."

In times of stress this always renews me. And I always feel the comfort, and often, joy. In those times I am reminded of Julian of Norwich, the 14th Century Christian mystic, whose spirituality and sense of joy and optimism flourished even in an era when the Christian theology was focused on sin and punishment, not joy.

"All will be well — all will be well," wrote Julian, in spite of the rigidity of her church.

At last, I think I understand my second grade nemesis, Sister Ellen Marie. Perhaps her own joyless life was simply a reflection of her earlier experiences and training. Somehow she got herself locked into the theology of the 14th Century. Are you listening, Sister Ellen Marie?

"All will be well. All will be well."

Indeed, all is well in my garden. Prayer doesn't always need words. Sometimes it is just heightened awareness. How do you put words around that? You don't have to.

Sometimes I even sing. But, *only* if I am sure no one can hear. Still, there is a high price to be paid for this. As soon as I open my mouth every single bird flies away.

Even so, each day in the garden one should laugh a little, sing a little, dance a little, and pray a little. And who's to say where one will end and the other begin.

Our pastor, Roy Howard, who has brought the vitality of his own deep spirituality to Saint Mark, has always stressed understanding prayer as "paying attention." For me, this has been his gift of validating my own internal prayer life, which I am not one to articulate in public. But that is okay, because I am a person who pays attention — some of the time.

Paying attention is a way of life for Christopher Jones, author of *Listen Pilgrim*. He tells the story of his life as a pilgrimage of meeting people wherever they are and touching their lives. Sometimes the touch is just listening, or some small act of caring. As he tells of his random encounters with the lonely, or hurting "poor poor" and the "rich poor," he refers to them all as the "Christ on the street." He truly lives his interpretation of

Christ's words: "Inasmuch as you have done it unto the least of these my brethren, you have done it unto me."

"We don't always know who's poor," reminds Christopher Jones, "and we don't always know who is the Christ on the street."

Sometimes in life, I might add, you need to be the Christ on the Street, and sometimes you just need to recognize him. And , sometimes like me, you figure it out years later.

Looking back, it was really such a simple thing. but, it wasn't simple to me. Not then. As a middle school student I suffered the pangs of wanting to be popular and cool. This was difficult because being a very childish looking twelve was not at all conducive to being cool. And this is not an age when kids are known for their sensitivity to each other.

The high spot of my week was always my afternoon at the riding school. Because I was the youngest student I always got to ride Pegasus, the old mare. She was my favorite and I always thought that I was hers, too.

I certainly wasn't the favorite of the other students, who were all *Senior* highs and incredibly wealthy, cool and popular. You know — the "popular" kids, the ones with no pimples and perfect hair. I, on the other hand, was just "the kid." Sometimes tolerated, sometimes not.

One bitterly cold January day I walked into the stable where all the "popular" kids were gathered, drinking cokes and sneaking cigarettes in the warm, cozy tack room. It had been a hard day for me and I briefly enjoyed the fantasy of joining them. We would all laugh and drink cokes. And I would even share a forbidden cigarette. Wrong.

"Run along, kid," someone called, followed by a chorus of laughter.

It was the final rotten moment of an already terrible day. At that moment I "knew" as only an unhappy adolescent can "know", that I was just a pathetic loser and nothing could change that. I also knew that I was never, *ever* going to be welcome in that warm tack room.

Holding back tears, I stumbled into the straw littered hall where Pegasus was crosstied. Pegasus snorted softly, waiting for the sugar cube I always brought her. And I put my arms around the old mare's neck and wept.

Shuffling footsteps behind me announced the arrival of Tommy, the old, alcoholic stable hand. The butt of many teenage jokes, Tommy was even less cool than me. But, when he was sober, I always liked to talk with him about the horses.

This time I didn't even turn to greet him. Tommy walked up behind me and quietly laid his hand on my head. He never said a word. I don't know how long we stood there. I only know that something magic happened, and I was okay.

Now I know that, for that moment, Tommy was the "Christ on the Street." Tommy was paying attention.

And that is who we are called to be. People who pay attention.

Paying attention is part of my job as a therapist. For me, it is the hardest, and the best job in the world. Every day I sit down with people and discuss life and death, sex and money, hurts and fears and disappointments.

For some, things never change. For most others, it does. But always, it matters.

And then I retire to the garden to be replenished.

How convenient that the brick path, which branches directly off the garden's central walkway, leads straight to the hammock. This is not an accident.

Nestled in the woodland area, under a canopy of dogwood and pine trees, and surrounded by ferns, the hammock is a gentle reminder to take the time to let go. To take the time to listen to the body's message: "I'm tired," isn't always easy for me. Sometimes I want to keep marching on, to plant one more flat of ground cover, to weed one more section of path, to tie up one more vine. This, I have discovered, more times than I care to admit, is the path to injury.

Gradually, I have been replacing the "marching on" philosophy with the "work your edge" philosophy I learned in yoga. One side of that edge is pain and injury; the other side is slacking off, and just not trying very hard. The edge lies between these two sides.

The edge is growth. The edge is not static; sometimes it is higher, sometimes lower. Your body knows. So listen. How high is not what matters. Working your edge is what matters. Being here now is what matters.

I rediscovered yoga after months of weight training with a fitness nazi, whose mantra was: "push, push, push . . . harder, harder, harder." John Schumacher, my yoga teacher, taught me to understand the "edge" in life. John is one of the finest hatha yoga teachers in the country. I was not one of his finest students. All too often, I was on the bottom side of the edge. Although, in retrospect, John would probably be surprised if he knew how much I learned from him, and how often I refer to it.

"Working the edge" is not exactly a buzzword in the contemporary culture of young professionals. For many, production and achievement are the primary goals. This leaves very little time for reflection and meditation. One of my friends describes herself this way: "I am a human doing, not a human being."

In our middle class suburbia we learn to be "human doings" from early childhood. Even young children are left little time for reflection, as they are raced from one educational or "enriching" activity to another.

It has just occurred to me that, by this standard, I was culturally deprived. I just never knew it. We did have family museum and art gallery visits, in addition to ballet and art lessons. But, other than that, my parents were not overly focused on "enrichment."

This worked out well for me. I had a lot of free time to spend playing with friends and amusing myself. My parents valued the independence of a child who rarely said: "I'm bored." So they were always happy to see me wander off, pulling my little red wagon. Often, I sat in that little wagon, pushing myself along with my feet, as I daydreamed, and just enjoyed nature.

We lived at the top of a long, gently sloping hill, which provided the perfect setting for a little daydreamer to lie down in her wagon and look up at the clouds as she slowly coasted down the hill.

Now, as a parent, I would question the wisdom of watching the clouds while you are rolling into traffic. But, I survived, and I have always been grateful that I had the opportunity and the free time to enjoy my little, red wagon.

*Marigold*

Today, the hammock is my little, red wagon. I have worked to my "edge" and it is time for a break. Although there is a mindful quality to each labor in the garden, I am tired now. The hammock is calling to me from its wooded glen. It is time to just "be" in the hammock.

Lying in the rope cradle of the hammock, beneath a leafy canopy, I can feel my arms and legs become relaxed and heavy. All tension slides away. The world around is quiet and green.

Then, as I quiet down, the sound of silence shifts, and I am aware of the emerging sounds of life all around me. Somewhere in the background is the constant drone of bees and chirping of crickets. From the pond comes the steady splash of water pouring over the falls and hitting the rock below. The birds can be heard chattering to each other in their communal bath above the pond.

Taking this time to pause in the garden and to be at one with the world around me never fails to stir in me a sense of wonder and awe. Buddhists would call this the "sacred pause" and would liken it to the experience of the Buddha when he stopped "doing," and simply sat under the bodhi tree and opened himself to "being."

And this is the pause to experience the gift of this day. And the pause to ask myself the question posed by the poet, Mary Oliver, a kindred spirit, who lives under her own bodhi tree. "What is it you plan to do with your one wild and precious life?"

**The Summer Day**
*Who made the world?*
*Who made the swan, and the black bear?*
*Who made the grasshopper?*
*This grasshopper, I mean*
*the one who has flung herself out of the grass,*
*the one who is eating sugar out of my hand,*
*who is moving her jaws back and forth instead of up and down,*

*who is gazing around with her enormous and complicated eyes.*
*Now she lifts her pale forearms and thoroughly washes her face.*
*Now she snaps her wings open, and floats away.*
*I don't know exactly what a prayer is.*
*I do know how to pay attention, how to fall down*
*into the grass, how to kneel down in the grass,*
*how to be idle and blessed, how to stroll through the fields,*
*which is what I have been doing all day.*
*tell me, what else should I have done?*
*Doesn't everything die at last, and too soon?*
*Tell me, what is it you plan to do*
*with your one wild and precious life?*
—Mary Oliver, *New and Selected Poems*

# CHAPTER 12

# *A Time to Build Up*

*We have forgotten who we are.*

*We have forgotten who we are*
*We have alienated ourselves from the movements*
*    of the earth*
*We have become estranged from the movements of*
*    the earth*
*We have turned our backs on the cycles of life.*

*We have forgotten who we are.*

*We have sought only our own security*
*We have exploited simply for our own ends*
*We have distorted our knowledge*
*We have abused our power*

*We have forgotten who we are.*

*Now the land is barren*
*And the waters are poisoned*
*And the air is polluted.*

*We have forgotten who we are.*

*Now the forests are dying*

*And the creatures are disappearing*
*And humans are despairing*

*We have forgotten who we are.*

*We ask forgiveness*
*We ask for the gift of remembering*
*We ask for the strength to change*

*We have forgotten who we are.*
—U.N. Environmental Sabbath Program

While I am lying in the hammock pondering what I plan to do with my "one wild and precious life," I have also begun to ponder the wild and precious life all around me.

Even in a one-acre garden it is apparent that all the wild, and not so wild, things in nature are interconnected and interdependent. Most of the little creatures are some bigger creature's food. If these insects and animals are destroyed or disappear, what will become of the bigger creatures for whom they are a major food source?

This is the balance of nature — predators and victims. Most of the predators are themselves, someone else's victim. I try not to think too much about this while I am actually in the hammock.

It is not all that comforting to realize that as you are swinging gently in the breeze, some little guy in the underbrush is about to have an appendage chewed off by a bigger guy, or that the lawn mower chugging in the front yard has just turned another toad into mush.

But the biggest predator of all is man. We are the enemy.

Most of us don't even reflect on this, as we continue to enjoy our urban-suburban sprawl with all the comforts of high tech living. Meanwhile, we are replacing wildlife habitat with concrete and neatly trimmed lawns, hybrid plants that will contain no seeds for wildlife to munch on, pesticides to eliminate "annoying" insects, not to mention detergents and

chemicals, all of which foul our land and our water supply. It seems that while we profess our love for God on the weekend, the rest of the week we are busy trashing His world.

Anne Raver has expressed this in a beautifully written book of essays, *Deep in the Green: An Exploration of Country Pleasures* (1995). She chronicles the increasing sprawl of building, preceded by bulldozers destroying still more woods, leaving even less land available to soak up the rain water. Thus, with the addition of our widespread use of fertilizers and pesticides, there occurs more and more toxic run-off, washing into our waterways.

The end result, Raver points out, will be the creation of new areas like Manhattan, creating ecological disasters where, as Raver puts it, "the only bodies swimming in the East River are dead ones." Numerous insightful authors such as Raver point out our dangerous and sometimes deadly mis-use of the world God has given us. How many times must we be told?

What happens, I am left to wonder, when the diseases and tumors that are now appearing in fish begin to appear on our own bodies? What, indeed?

In Genesis, the first book of the Bible, God tells Adam and Eve to "be fruitful and multiply and fill the earth and subdue it, and have dominion over the fish of the sea and over the birds of the air, and over every living thing that moves upon the earth."

Well, we got the first part right. We have been fruitful. And God knows, we have multiplied. But we blew the next part. Having dominion over the earth means stewardship, not ownership. Over the last century we have been poor stewards of the earth. Our grandchildren will pay the price.

My own ecological awakening was further stirred by Sara Stein, author of *Noah's Garden*, who lamented:

> I'm lucky to have spent my childhood summers among woods, streams, meadows, and marshes, but most suburbanites have never searched for frogs' eggs, caught fireflies in a jar, or peeked into a grassy nest of adorable baby mice. As the years pass, fewer and

fewer people will long for the call of bullfrogs. Today's children growing up on lawns and pavements will not even have nostalgia to guide them, and soon the animals will be not only missing but forgotten.

The "Noah's Garden" concept of "restoring the ecology of our own backyards" fueled my excitement about creating habitat in our own garden. Now we have become one more link with thousands of other Americans across the country, whose garden habitats shelter wildlife and provide necessary food and shelter pit stops for migrating birds and butterflies.

That is why the path that leads to the hammock also passes the bird condo community. Situated on a curving needle path that winds off the main brick path, a collection of tired, brown bird houses is mounted on 4 x 4 posts. Nestled together in the clearing, they form a contemporary, avian, moderate income housing unit.

The more affluent bird accommodations are located in a group of colorful villas mounted along the back fence behind the children's park. Individual bird houses and feeders are scattered throughout the garden.

The bird census continues to mount. This is partly because in our suburban county the woodland areas continue to shrink, so we can build even more houses and condos, widen more roads, and build more shopping centers. Goodbye, habitat. The other reason is that we are very good landlords. Food, water and shelter are always in plentiful supply here.

Like the woodland hammock area, the moderate income housing area is densely under-planted with small shrubs and ground cover plants to provide a healthy habitat for the birds. All manner of creeping, crawling little insects and spiders have made this under-story their sanctuary. Little do they know that while they are experiencing this as their sanctuary, the birds are preparing to experience them as a buffet.

Much of the ground cover planting here would be considered unimaginative by landscape designers. This is because the whole area is thick with pachysandra and periwinkle, both of which are staples in every garden center across the country. There is a reason for that.

They may not be original but they sell. This is because they work. Periwinkle, otherwise known as vinca minor, is the more beautiful of the

two. It has glossy leaves on trailing stems, and in the early springtime is covered with masses of blue-purple blossoms.

Pachysandra, or Japanese spurge, is the hardier and more versatile of the two. It will tolerate more poor treatment and considerably deeper shade. Both propagate well, but pachysandra is more prolific in that regard. It spreads by underground rhizomes to form a dense, evergreen mat. On rainy days I frequently go to an established patch of pachysandra and gently pull out several plants, complete with trailing root systems. Once transplanted in a new area, they will soon form a new colony.

For a brief period I had great success using Virginia creeper as a quick and easy solution to covering large, bald areas in the garden. One barren patch of dry soil near the back fence had successfully killed every plant that had ever tried to live there.

Then, enter the Virginia creeper vine. It can grow in sun or shade, drought or flood, poor soil, or rich compost. This should have been a warning. Soon the bare fence was hidden under a multitude of little branches, all covered with soft green leaves, all looking like fat, little green hands creeping up the boards.

Suddenly, the branches were snaking all across the ground. Some appeared yards away; others sneaked under and around existing shrubs. My success story was turning into the garden version of flesh-eating bacteria. Every time I pulled out a handful of creeper vines there would be a long, trailing mass of vines to follow.

I was starting to feel like one of those clowns who keeps pulling handkerchiefs out of his pocket. They are always attached to other handkerchiefs, and on, and on, and on. This could be the plant that ate Potomac. At any rate, after spending the better part of a summer trying to eradicate it, I feel qualified to issue fair warning. Virginia creeper is the plant from Hell.

The birds and insects are not the only beneficiaries of all this ground cover. It also provides the benefit of keeping shrub roots cool and protected during the hot, dry summer months. Better yet, when established, a good ground cover virtually eliminates weeds. Even without the habitat benefit, eliminating weeds would be a good enough reason to justify its existence.

A lot has been written about the zen of weeding and its great therapeutic value. I have done a lot of weeding, and for me, the therapeutic value wears off rather quickly. This may be different for those who have reached a higher level of enlightenment.

With the addition of a smaller, mini-pond below the condo units, the birds have the extra benefit of bathing and drinking right at their doorstep. Now, the toads and frogs are beginning to arrive in greater numbers. This is good news for the garden. Bad news for the insects.

As the finishing touch, the entry path to the bird condo is graced with a stone statue of "Saint Stan." Actually, the statue's inscription indicates that he is Saint Fiacre, the patron saint of gardening. But, we know better.

Everyone who knew my husband in his bearded days agrees that the statue of the saint, standing in his long robe, carrying his ever present shovel, is a dead ringer for Stan.

Minus the robe, of course. The day I spied the good saint at the Good Earth Garden Center, I knew he would have to come home with me.

Not to be outdone, Stan turned up the following Christmas with the perfect present for me: a serene, winged angel, who now gazes beneficently out from the azalea path. Stan insists that she looks like me. She doesn't. And that is the really "perfect" part. He thinks she does.

The birds are delighted with their multitude of houses, feeders, ponds, and habitat of shrubs and trees. As landlords, we even provide peanut butter, generously smeared on trees and stumps. This provides fat and protein for high energy. When you're a bird you never know when you may need a quick burst of energy to escape a predator.

Henry Mitchell, author of *The Essential Earth Man*, recognized this. "The only problem with birds," he pointed out, "is that they attract cats." And the only drawback to this bird Eden has been the presence of our neighbor's cats.

"Boots," the major villain, was a narcissistic, testosterone-laden death machine for the birds. He was also a shameless schmoozer. After committing murder and mayhem in the garden, Boots always came around to rub against my leg and purr softly.

At first, I tried to modify Boots' behavior by providing a saucer of

milk and some tasty snacks. In theory, I reasoned, a full cat is a passive cat. Wrong. Boots ate my snacks, drank my saucers of milk, and *then* killed my birds.

Occasionally, when Boots was feeling kindly, he would repay my generosity with a little gift of his own. These tokens of appreciation he provided by depositing on my doorstep a severed body part from his latest victim.

Receiving these peace offerings from Boots is just a reminder that, in the natural order of things, he is no different than the birds he victimized. They would gladly suck up a poor earthworm, who is just going about his business enriching the soil.

Certainly, he is no more immoral than the men who disturb this balance by calling themselves "hunters." They put on silly hats, hundreds of dollars worth of L.L. Bean's finest, and march off into the woods to kill animals they don't need. And sometimes, like Boots, they bring home trophies to display their manhood.

In the world of nature, all this carnage, when uninterrupted, begins to even out. The predators and victims strike a balance, and all the species survive. Although the unlucky ones still end up as someone's dinner, the system works. We have been watching this play out in our own little ecosystem.

For a long time our garden suffered from an onslaught of rabbits. At first, they were adorable. It was not at all unusual to walk along the garden path and hear a sudden rustle in the brush. If you turned quickly you would be in time to see the white underside of a fluffy-tail, as its owner bounded off into the deeper brush. Other times, the rabbit would sit motionless, eyeing you with big dark eyes, silently willing you to leave so he could finish his lunch in peace.

Soon the rabbits became less timid. Although they still kept a watchful eye out, their attitude shifted to "ho, hum, it's another human in our garden." Yawn. And all the while they appeared to be multiplying every few weeks. Even after watching all our young azaleas get chewed to the nubs by the voracious bunnies, I still could not bring myself to hurt one of these cuddly creatures. I have too many happy memories of my childhood pet, "Hoppy."

Instead, I tried the diversion method. Using bags of fresh carrots to mark the way, I made a trail leading from the tastiest, young azaleas to the compost pile. Here, I decided, the rabbits could safely munch on the remains of our left-over table salads.

It soon became clear that this method left much to be desired. The azaleas were, if anything, looking worse than ever. Mary, my sister-in-law, did not even have the decency to hide her laughter.

"Alice," she pointed out. "What if some of the rabbits were starting at the compost pile? Now your carrot trail has led them right to the azaleas."

Soon that was no longer an issue. Because, as the naturalists maintain, if you have the food source a predator likes, he will come. And come he did. Late one night, as I looked out over our floodlit deck, there on the edge stood a magnificent, young, red fox.

He stood there proudly, almost as if he was aware that this was a "Kodak moment," Motionless, he continued to sniff the air. It was a beautiful thing to watch — if you could forget that he was on his way to murder.

Since that night the red fox appears to have taken up residence in the garden. There are still rabbits about, but no longer do they number in the hordes. And the occasional appearance of small tufts of brown and white fluff along the path bear silent witness to his skill.

The ecosystem really works. When you stop using the pesticides that kill not only the creatures you wish to eliminate, but randomly destroy every other living thing that chances upon that chemical, or eats the creature that ingested that poison, nature will take over and do the job for you.

Our hostas are living proof of this theory. Several years ago we planted an assorted selection of these large-leafed, shade-loving beauties along the woodland path. The result was awesome. It was stunning to see the effect of the many different shades of green all massed together.

The slugs were awed, too. They appeared out of nowhere and quickly managed to reproduce themselves many times over, while simultaneously

reducing the hosta population to shreds. The surviving plants were riddled with enough holes to totally alter the appearance of the once beautiful hosta bed. The tattered bed now resembled nothing so much as a mass of large, ratty, green doilies.

It is embarrassing as a gardener to admit that I resorted to a "better living through chemistry" phase. At first, liberal doses of Sluggo pellets, the snail and slug pesticide, did a masterful job of wiping out the slugs and allowing my hostas to rejuvenate themselves.

I don't even want to think about what it also did to the earth and to the ground water. Ironically, in a matter of months, the slugs apparently developed an immunity to the pesticide. They came roaring back with a renewed appetite.

Slugs are probably the most repulsive creatures on earth. You have to ask yourself what God had in mind when he created this slime covered glob of snot. Maybe He was just annoyed after Adam and Eve got kicked out of the Garden. So He tossed out a few slugs.

"Here, see how you like this. Maybe the next time you'll listen when I tell you not to touch something."

On the other hand, maybe in His infinite wisdom, He planned the slugs as a nutritional snack for some other species. I prefer that explanation. I wonder, though, why they couldn't be more attractively packaged.

When I came to my chemical senses the first line of defense was the salt shaker. As every gardener knows, if you go out on a rainy night with a flash light and a salt shaker you will find a multitude of these little slime balls sliding across the patio and the walkways.

One quick pour of salt and the gray slime ball turns into a white coated, writhing, oozing mass, as all the moisture is sucked from its body. In the morning, all that remains is a dried-out gray membrane stuck to the brick.

It works, but I cannot stomach it. Reducing any living creature to a writhing mass makes me feel like the predator I do not choose to be. And heaven knows, I am not going to eat it.

So, goodbye salt. Hello, grapefruit rinds. Basically, this method entails setting out grapefruit rinds at night. In the morning you will discover

the rinds crawling with slugs. This is not a pretty sight. It suggests sleeping late and hoping that your husband will get up first and make the discovery for himself.

I am not even going to discuss the disposal part.

The most successful man-made slug exterminator proved to be the small, empty tuna fish cans, which I filled with beer and sank in the ground at night. The slugs, simpletons that they were, plopped in for a beer before they realized that they couldn't swim. At least it was a more pleasant death than salt.

Chloe, our dog, loved this method of slug control. She was a huge great dane with a relatively tiny brain. With her giant body, shiny, black coat, and pointed ears, Chloe was often mistaken for a gargantuan doberman. One repair man would not enter the house until the dog was banished to the yard.

"That is the doberman from hell," was his description. Actually, "Suzy Cream Cheese" would have been a more accurate way to describe her. Chloe was a warm, loving schmoozer of a dog. Still, she probably shouldn't have tried to put her paws on his shoulders and lick him to death.

Early one morning Chloe got out in the garden before I was up. When I called her for breakfast she did not show up. This was not like our chow hound. Concerned, I searched through the garden until I found Chloe, lying quietly in a patch of dappled sunlight, snoring softly. As I approached, Chloe lifted a sleepy head, opened one eye and gently belched.

After a few more breakfasts of warm beer and dead slugs, we feared that Chloe might soon need to enter a recovery program. It was time to find a new method of slug control.

Ecologically speaking, the answer was there all along. We just didn't see it. It was as simple as a water-filled bag of tadpoles, which were dumped unceremoniously into the garden pond one summer afternoon.

The original tadpoles are now well into the great-grandparent generation. Their extended family members are everywhere. The slugs are nowhere. And the hostas are radiant again. All's right with the world.

Our garden is now filled with even more frogs and toads, who have gotten the message that this is the happy hunting ground. Even Fred, the

grouchy turtle, who somehow lost his mate, Dolores, has found some new buddies. He has been joined by Ariel and Travis, who were gifted by Second Chance, a rescue group that rehabilitates injured wildlife. They saved the turtles from a near road kill and sent them to us for foster parenting.

Travis is now fat and happy in his new home. At least, I think he is fat. He has an awfully big shell. Although Ariel is still reticent about public appearances, Travis is occasionally spotted sidling across one of the brick paths. He usually picks up speed when he sees me coming.

Because Travis appears to be fearless around humans, I assume that he experienced a lot of caring and handling while he was recovering at Second Chance. He is not afraid of us. He just doesn't like us very much.

At first, Travis will endure being picked up, and meets me eye-to-eye with his beady, little, red-eyed stare. Soon he has had enough and begins to make little swimming motions with his feet.

"Unhand me, you great, ugly human," he appears to be thinking.

Reluctantly, I set Travis down on the path again, but not before making my parting shot:

"After all I've done for you—," I remind him, as he lumbers off. Travis doesn't care.

As for Ariel . . . Fred may just have found himself a new bride. Who knows? Fred's not talking.

But what is to become of the Freds of the world if the bulldozers keep coming and more and more of the woodlands and wetlands disappear? In this country, as in the rest of the world, we are witnessing governments sanctioning the continued exploitation of the earth's natural resources.

"Smart growth" has become the new buzz word for developers and local governments as they mow down more and more forests to build yet another highway or shopping center. Gone are the trees that would cleanse the air by absorbing carbon dioxide, and reduce erosion by absorbing and slowing down storm water that could refill the wetlands and raise the water table rather than ending up as wasted runoff. Gone is habitat.

"Smart growth" is frequently not too smart. It is just another euphemism for destroying the earth in the name of "smart economic growth."

Just ask Ariel and Travis, who nearly got mashed on a smart growth highway to another smart growth shopping center, where we can all buy more things we don't need.

Just when I am feeling helpless about the steady destruction of the earth, something usually happens to restore my hope. Recently, it was picking up the *Washington Post* and reading the inspiring article by DeNeen L. Brown about the Ojibway Indian tribe in Manitoba, Canada.

The Poplar River First Nation is an Ojibway tribe who inhabit a portion of the 13 billion acre Boreal Forest. Scientists call the Boreal one-half of the earth's "lungs." The remaining half is the Amazon Rain Forest on the other end of the world.

Working together, Ms. Brown explained, the two lungs absorb the excess carbon dioxide and release oxygen. Without these lungs to remove millions of tons of carbon dioxide, the ensuing green house effect could accelerate the process of global warming.

Naturally, "smart growth" is not limited to the United States. The developers are already breathing hard to enter the Boreal so they can cut trees, build roads, mine for gas and oil, and build massive hydropower dams. Just what the world needs.

In return for access to the forest, the wealthy developers have promised the kind of money that could change the modest lifestyle of the Ojibway to a more progressive way of life.

But, the tribe view their land as not only a source of livelihood, but as a spiritual connection to the earth. The elders have held firm. Money, they feel, is something you have and spend. The land is forever.

Hooray for the Ojibway tribe! They have truly grasped the message of the First Testament. The earth is ours to care for, not to lay waste to. It is a sacred trust.

The sacred trust is a good beginning. As voters we have the power to send a message to the lawmakers that they need to uphold this trust—whether or not they personally endorse it. Not. The developers have more money with which to pressure the lawmakers. We need to use the pressure of the vote.

The best way to get excited about it is to start in our own backyards. It's all so easy, really, if all the homeowners across the land would become excited about dedicating part of their land for the creation of habitat. And all the gardeners were to see themselves as stewards of the land. Maybe then, in some small way, we could begin to rebuild—not one high-rise at a time, or one mall at a time—but one garden at a time.

Then there would still be time to teach our children, if they are to save the world for their children. The Native Americans always knew this. Why didn't we?

> *Teach your children*
> *what we have taught our children—*
> *that the earth is our mother.*
> *Whatever befalls the earth*
> *befalls the sons and daughters of the earth.*
> *If men spit upon the ground,*
> *they spit upon themselves.*
>
> *This we know.*
> *The earth does not belong to us,*
> *we belong to the earth.*
> *This we know.*
> *All things are connected*
> *like the blood which unites one family.*
> *All things are connected.*
>
> *Whatever befalls the earth*
> *befalls the sons and daughters of the earth.*
> *We did not weave the web of life.*
> *We are merely a strand in it.*
> *Whatever we do to the web,*
> *we do to ourselves.*
> —Chief Seattle

CHAPTER 13

# A *Thyme*
# *to Heal*

*By Grace divine, not otherwise*
*O Nature, We are thine.*
—William Wordsworth

Thyme To Heal" reads the carved message over the arched entry to the herb garden. The three 4 x 8 foot long raised beds occupy one of the few sunny places in our woodland garden. The beds are joined by whiskey half-barrels for the mint and lemon balm plants and enclosed by hollies and rhododendrons to form a small, sunny room.

It is ironic that a cooking-challenged person like myself would love the herb garden so much. What turns me on is the smell of the sun-warmed herbs and the bursts of bright colors from the geraniums, petunias, marigolds and black-eyed susans that pop up between the herbs.

In future years I plan to become, if not Julia Child, at least a culinary artist. But, for now, my artistic energies are being channeled into learning to play the cello. Julia Child will just have to wait. I can only create so many new neural pathways at a time. In the meantime, even fast food tastes better with herbs.

So, the herb garden of today is limited to a few old faithful stand-bys. At the top of the list is mint. There are a multitude of flavored mint plants, but I prefer spearmint and peppermint. Spearmint is stronger, but peppermint appears to repel some insects, as well as smelling wonderful in floral arrangements.

In the summer months our refrigerator is always stocked with large jugs of chilled water, garnished with lemon slices and fresh mint. Delicious. My good friend, Dot, shared many happy hours with me in the gazebo, sipping frosted glasses of minted ice tea. Later, during some less happy hours in her life, she would remind me of those good times.

Running out of mint is never a problem for the herb gardener. These plants give new meaning to the term "hardy perennial." Left to their own devices, mint plants will gladly fill the entire herb bed. The long roots spread rapidly under the soil and soon little mint-lets are popping up all over the garden.

Planting the mint in a plastic growers' pot and sinking the pot in the earth so just the top edge of the pot is slightly above the soil will solve the problem. Our solution was to assign them a whiskey half-barrel of their own where they can flourish in abandon.

The other whiskey half-barrel in the herb garden has been assigned to the lemon balm plants, a main staple of the herb beds. I did not choose it to be a staple at all. The lemon balm chose itself. That is why it was banished to the whiskey barrel.

Rampant growth is an understatement. This plant would be happy to choke out every other herb in the bed. This makes it the herbal equivalent of Virginia creeper. But, in return for all this aggravation, lemon balm smells wonderfully fresh and lemony. It tastes delicious in iced tea and, when rubbed on the arms, repels insects.

Dill is an annual worth growing just for its decorative attributes. Growing up to three feet tall, it is light and airy and adds a flair to any bouquet. When chopped up and added to softened butter, dill makes a very tasty spread. In fact, anything with butter, or pasta, is vastly improved with dill.

Dot, who shared many a summer lunch in the garden, once observed that my lack of cooking skills frequently has been cleverly concealed by my talent for re-arranging pre-prepared foods in an artistic fashion and adding the flourish of herbal garnishes. Presentation is everything. Well, not really.

Oregano is tall with mounded, dark green leaves and a pungent flavor that screams "Italian." All the stereotypical, spicy, Italian fast foods incorporating pizza, spaghetti and tomato-based sauces, feature oregano. Some herbal reference books claim that oregano also possesses great healing qualities for the treatment of spider bites.

Now there is a piece of information I could have used a few years ago, when a trip to the garden shed netted me a nasty bite from a brown recluse spider. The culprit had been lurking in a dark corner of the shed and somehow managed to slide down the back of my shirt.

Prior to this experience, I had retained the "good spider" feelings from my younger days when I had enjoyed reading, "Charlotte's Web." That delightful children's book left me with the view that "Mrs. Spider is your friend." Your friend, maybe. Not mine.

For me, any friendship with Mrs. Spider is going to be a long distance one. And I am even conflicted about that. Apparently, I am one of those persons for whom the bite of a brown recluse spider is highly toxic.

The initial bite produced a fever and a large, deep, ulcerated wound. The oozing, open wound would not heal and steadily grew larger. Feeling increasingly sick, but nonetheless resisting an emergency room visit, I compounded the problem by going to a nearby "doc-in-a-box" clinic. Big mistake.

I am not multi-lingual so I have a strong preference for doctors who speak English. I also prefer medical school graduates. This gentleman did not appear to fit in either category. The only word I could grasp sounded like "hmm-m-m." I thought only people in my profession said things like that. He did manage to convey the message that he had no idea what the problem was. He then proceeded to prescribe a medicine to which I am allergic.

I never found out whether oregano would have provided a cure. The wound was not healing, and I preferred the safety of known medicine. With ongoing care from my own "real" doctor, the bite eventually healed, but it was a long, unpleasant process.

Hopefully, I can learn to adopt a more environmentalist attitude toward the spider, who is, after all, just acting like a spider in the whole

ecological balance of life. But, bad sport that I am, I still harbor some resentment toward the brown recluse, who clearly is not to be trusted.

Rosemary, a really beautiful, small evergreen shrub, is another herb with reputed medicinal properties. I am very partial to rosemary for its clean, refreshing, almost pine-like scent. It is especially soothing when you put a few snips of rosemary in a gauze bag with some lavender and drop them in a warm tub. Soak in this for 20 minutes and you will forget that you ever had any problems.

The herbalists say that according to historical lore, rosemary is for remembrance. It was once used in bridal bouquets, and for funeral arrangements. Early Greek scholars wore wreathes of rosemary while studying.

Rosemary is also the component of some of the medications used for rheumatism. It is touted for helping with digestion. If you want a pleasant way to check that out, try some roast lamb garnished with rosemary, or some lightly buttered new potatoes sprinkled gently with rosemary. Aromatic and delicious, this is a test you may want to keep repeating.

After trying the herbalist recommendation that oil of rosemary when rubbed into the temples can relieve a headache, I am a believer. I have been informed by a well respected doctor that this is merely the placebo effect. That's okay, it works for me.

Thyme is a delightful, little, aromatic, evergreen herb. We use the creeping version which has little, bitty grayish-green leaves and crawls between the cobblestones in the pergola. It makes a soft ground cover that is faintly aromatic when walked upon. Thyme is a piquant, tasty addition to most soups. I find that the soup tastes better if I don't focus on the fact that someone was recently walking on the ingredients.

Parsley is probably the most common of all the herbs. Almost any food can be improved by the addition of a bit of parsley chopped into it, or sprigged on top of it. Curly parsley is my favorite. It is also the favorite for the butterflies in their larval stage. So, we always put a few parsley plants in the butterfly bed as host plants for the butterflies of tomorrow.

Italian parsley is taller with flatter leaves, and has more flavor. It is generally preferred by the more sophisticated cooks. Of course, I had to put a couple Italian parsley plants in the herb beds. I like to keep my culinary options open. But, I still prefer the curly ones.

Chives are the delicate relatives of the onion family. The long, slender leaves can be chopped up in almost any entré dish. At least they can when I am cooking. In the late spring the chive plant is topped with delicate, little purplish-pink, ball-shaped blossoms. I find them too pretty to snip off and allow them to remain in the bed, blooming their little hearts out. This may be to the detriment of the remaining leaves, but that, I think, is a small price to pay.

As a young bride it was chives, parsley and rosemary that saved me from disgrace with my new in-laws.

My husband comes from a Pennsylvania German family of great cooks. Frequently, their cooking involved the use of enough saturated fat to clog the arteries of an elephant. But, it certainly was tasty.

For them, to relinquish their first born son to the arms of a culinary-challenged woman was probably on a par with a family in the early days of India's history, discovering that their son's bride-to-be had no dowry. Fortunately, the Pennsylvania Germans are not into bride burning. Nonetheless, as a new bride the expectation level was high, and the talent level was low.

One weekend when my in-laws announced on short notice that they would be arriving for a brief visit I knew that at least one good meal was in order. I briefly considered visiting a local restaurant with one of my large, ceramic casserole pans in tow. With a suitable bribe, I figured the chef could fill it with something appropriate.

The results might well be quite impressive. At the same time I presented my gastronomic masterpiece, I could also demonstrate how well I was using the pretty casserole pans, which were part of a cooking set that was a wedding gift from the Pennsylvania relatives. Those Pennsylvania Germans know what's important.

Ultimately, I resorted to a slightly less blatant form of subterfuge. In a

large pan I sauteed chives, parsley, rosemary, celery and onions, all swimming in several sticks of melted butter. Quite aromatic. Then, in went several cans of Dinty Moore Beef Stew. The crowning touch was a bottle of my finest red wine. No ordinary cooking wine for this feast. Let it be noted that at this point in my marriage the standard for "finest" wine was not very high.

When we all sat down to dinner everyone proclaimed that this was a truly fine meal. Everyone had seconds! I had arrived. It was eat, drink and be merry time. And thank God for the herbs.

Herbs can be gathered at any time of day, and mine frequently are. If you are a purist, though, you will harvest them early in the morning hours when they are still at their peak.

Sometimes, on warm summer mornings, I do remember to harvest a small bunch of herbs before the sun has had a chance to bake out some of their oily, aromatic essence. The resulting herbal bouquet is placed to soak in a small pewter pitcher on the kitchen sink. There, the herbs happily scent the room as they await their turn to be added to the day's meals.

It is easy to air dry the remaining herbs for future use. They are tied into small bundles and hung to dry in the darkened herb house. Once dry, the herbs can be chopped into small bits and stored in airtight containers.

The herb house is one of my all time favorite Christmas presents. Stan arranged delivery of the little 8 x 10 wooden frame house — it is much too charming to be called a shed. It arrived shortly after Christmas and was assembled by a small group of Amish builders.

Complete with screened windows, shutters, and cupola, the little house settled in next to the butterfly garden and soon appeared to have been there forever. Always one to skirt the edge of "gilding the lily," I added a colorful rug and a small "antique" table and chairs.

"Alice," commented one of my friends, "only you would have antiques and an oriental rug in your shed."

I beg to differ. This is *not* a shed. It is an herb *house*, And, actually, the "antique" table is a Miller original, created from an ancient treadle sewing machine base we found in a woodland dump behind a Pennsylvania farm.

A new "old" table top was fashioned from the top of an aging cherry wood table that was rescued from the same location.

The "oriental" rug dates back to the early marriage era, and probably has never been closer to the orient than Newark, New Jersey. But the resulting ambiance within the herb house has made it a sought-after space for changing into swim suits, or just as a children's special hang-out.

If you are a child, the herb house is a wonderful place to meet in secret and to share things not meant for adult ears. And, best of all, it is the ultimate scene for the inclusion-exclusion rites of childhood.

"Go away! This is the boys' house. No girls allowed!" Slam.

Life has a way of evening out these little injustices. Soon enough, the tables will be turned. Sometimes, of course, a little parental intervention is involved.

In the midst of all the other activities, the herb house still remains as the primary place for drying herbs. In the beginning of my herb collection days I kept going into the herb house to assess my bounty, only to find loose herbs strewn on the floor beneath the bundles hanging from the rafters. The resulting debris on my "oriental" carpet was messy, labor intensive, and became increasingly annoying.

"What dirty rodent has been sneaking in here?" I muttered to myself as I re-tied the bundles and vowed dire consequences for the culprit.

I would prefer not to admit how many times I re-tied those herb bundles before it finally dawned on me that, as the herbs dried they also shrank. The string, once firmly tied, loosened up, and the herbs gradually slipped out and dropped to the floor. A supply of rubber bands quickly solved that problem.

My herb harvesting is still on a small scale and not always by the book. I understand the importance of not allowing the herbs to go to flower and then to seed, which will then reduce the quality of the leaf. But, I am willing to sacrifice the quality of some of the plants in order to let the flowering occur.

The butterflies love the flowering tops of some of the herbs, especially the spearmint. And I love the butterflies. That seems like a worthwhile trade-off.

When the butterflies come to your garden you will know that all is right with your world. As a measure of your garden's environmental health, the butterfly is like the canary in the coal mine. Ever sensitive to pesticides and chemicals, these fragile creatures cannot survive in a toxic environment.

Our original butterfly bed was recently made more aesthetically beautiful when we added azaleas, crape myrtle, and hydrangeas to further enhance the beauty of the marigolds, sedum, salvia, astilbe and verbena that the butterflies love.

As the trees and shrubs grew, so also did the amount of shade in the garden. The butterflies did not find that more aesthetically beautiful at all. They need the warmth and light of the full sun for at least six hours a day.

This is not a problem for the butterflies. As the afternoon shade appears in the butterfly bed, they simply migrate over to the herb beds, which remain in full sun for most of the day.

Much of my understanding of the butterflies came from visiting La Ferme Des Papillions in the French West Indies. Located back in the hills in a remote part of the island, the butterfly farm is an enchanting experience. Well, it was enchanting once we got there. Getting there was not quite so enchanting.

The big drawback was a long, hot ride on a typical, rundown, island bus that appeared to be held together with baling wire and staples. The bus complained loudly with each shift of the gears and was grindingly in need of a lube job.

None of this bothered our chatty bus driver, though. Clearly, *he* was already well lubricated. As we boarded the bus, the driver told us his name and cheerfully announced that his drink of choice was pina colada. After the stopover, he informed us, the last person to re-enter the bus was to bring him another pina colada.

I wanted to be the last one on, just so I could *not* bring him a pina colada. I would gladly have sprung for a double cappucino.

The roads in Saint Martin are not exactly in pristine condition. As the bus careened over the winding, hilly roads, I couldn't help but notice that

the narrow roads also lacked the little niceties like shoulders and guard rails. This is not a good time to know that your driver has a snoot full of pina colada.

"I can live without seeing the butterflies," I told Stan. "I just want to live, period."

However, as Stan pointed out, getting off the bus now was not really an option.

Since I did live, I decided that visiting the butterfly farm was worth it after all. At first glance, the farm is just a compound of ragtag outbuildings atop a sun filled, grassy hill in the middle of nowhere.

The compound and surrounding grounds are completely enclosed with wire mesh screening. The enclosed space, sunny, warm and humid, is filled with tropical plants and thousands of beautiful, brightly colored butterflies. Flying in every direction and occasionally alighting on an outstretched arm, the butterflies displayed a dazzling array of markings and colors. It gave new meaning to the word "awesome."

Run by a small group of dedicated naturalists, the butterfly farm exists to further the preservation of rare species, and to provide the public with a better understanding of the world of butterflies and their need for habitat.

The butterflies, they explained, need the sun's warmth if they are to fly and search for nectar and water. Providing a large, flat rock in the sun will give the butterflies a place to land, and also allow them to absorb heat from the warm rock. Without heat, the butterflies are unable to fly.

Water for the butterflies, we learned, is not going to come from a full bird bath or a large body of water. Too scary if you are a butterfly. You could quickly become waterlogged. They like to "drink" the moisture from damp, muddy soil or wet sand. The perfect watering hole is a shallow basin filled with sand and then liberally watered.

Nectar for food comes from a wide array of sources: astilbe, verbena, sedum, petunias, the single flowers of impatiens, black-eyed susans, french marigolds, butterfly weed, butterfly bush, and many flowering shrubs, just to name a few.

In the larval stage the butterflies depend on host plants like milkweed, queen anne's lace, dogwood, and parsley. When you consider the

*Black-Eyed Susan*

end result, a few holes chewed by caterpillars in the host plants seems like a small price to pay.

After chemicals and insecticides, the biggest threat for butterflies comes from their major predator, the birds. Nature has come to the rescue of the vulnerable butterflies by providing them with wildly beautiful colors and markings, which are designed to confuse the birds. Remember, there is a reason for the term "bird brain."

Never, ever touch a butterfly, we were cautioned. Human touch is a death sentence. The wing colors also serve as a protective coating. Those colors are easily rubbed off. Then, when the rain comes, the wings will become waterlogged. When that happens the butterfly can no longer fly and will soon die.

To watch the butterflies flit through the garden is a purely joyous experience. They always remind me to stop everything for just a moment and feel grateful. And when I do, I recognize all over again the healing quality of gratitude. You just can't be miserable and grateful at the same time.

This is the reminder of gratitude in the Jewish ritual of the Passover service. "It would have been enough. . . ."

Of course, there is that very human part in all of us that says, "Well, yeah, that was really great, but I could use a little more." Recently, a friend shared one of his favorite jokes with that very message:

> *A Jewish grandma and her grandson are at the beach. He's playing in the water, she is standing on the shore not wanting to get her feet wet, when all of a sudden, a huge wave appears from nowhere and crashes directly onto the spot where the boy is wading. The water recedes and the boy is no longer there. He was swept away.*
>
> *The grandma holds her hands to the sky, screams and cries:*
> *"Lord, how could you?*
> *Haven't I been a wonderful grandmother?*
> *Haven't I been a wonderful mother?*

> *Haven't I kept a kosher home?*
> *Haven't I given to the B'nai B'rith?*
> *Haven't I lit candles every Friday night?*
> *Haven't I tried my very best to live a life that you would be proud of?"*
> *A voice booms from the sky. "All right already!"*
> *A few minutes later another huge wave appears out of nowhere and crashes on the beach. As the water recedes, the boy is standing there. He is smiling and splashing around as if nothing had ever happened.*
> *The voice booms again. "I have returned your grandson. Are you satisfied?"*
> *The grandma responds. "He had a hat."*

Jewish grandmothers don't have any monopoly on this attitude. We all want just a little more. And we all want the good stuff to go on forever.

The garden reminds us that life is full of love and beauty, but it is also about loss and death. I'm not always so good with that part. I prefer to recall my happiest garden memories, which include good friends like Dot, sharing those moments with me.

I will always remember one happy, sunny day when Dot accompanied me to the garden center to help select the two biggest, fattest, most beautifully shaped rhododendrons in the nursery. They were both to be incredibly lovely and perfectly symmetrical, to complement the new planter boxes, which flanked the entry to the sun room.

It was a day of fun and laughter. So much laughter that when we carried the new plants into the patio, Dot was still laughing so hard that she dropped hers. As soon as the big rhododendron thumped to the ground we knew that its symmetrical days were over.

When returned to an upright position there appeared a large gap on one side where two of the major branches had been snapped off.

We planted the two, now irregular, shrubs and laughed some more. Now, several years later, the large, healthy rhododendron still sits in its planter looking all lopsided and happy, reminding me of that delightful day.

Soon afterwards, Dot was diagnosed with colon cancer. The resulting surgery was painful and debilitating. All of Dot's good friends hoped and prayed for her recovery. As did Dot, but she also accepted that there are no guarantees.

"I don't want to die," she told her friends, "but I am not afraid."

Although she had never espoused the zen approach to life, Dot, nonetheless, was a living embodiment of that approach: "We cannot change what is. We can change our response." Dot's response was to continue to live her life in the fullest way possible.

From that point on, Dot began to experience living her life with a special kind of grace. It was as if she had a heightened sense of the value and beauty of each day.

Appropriately enough, grace was the topic of one of Roy's recent sermons, which opened with a reference to that common, but not-so-delicate, bumper sticker which reads "Shit happens." I think Roy added a gentler modification, like "Excrement occurs." But everyone got the point.

The more important point being that grace, that unexpected, life-enriching gift, happens. And probably more frequently than the former, but less often recognized. Grace happens.

And, when grace happens, it is important to recognize it. With gratitude. My first awareness of grace came when I was much too young to know the word. But I certainly felt the gratitude.

Little children who witness loud, angry outbursts from a parent generally perceive the fault to be theirs. So, perplexed and unhappy when my father's temper flared up yet again, I would retreat to the sunny back room and join my doll family. They could always be counted on to remain quiet and predictable.

Jackie, the life-sized "dummy," would always be sitting in his little rocking chair, awaiting my arrival. Jackie, who had begun his existence sitting on the lap of a ventriloquist, now provided a lap for me.

Curled up on Jackie's lap, with his stringy, cotton arms placed around me, I could gaze out at the sunny yard and pretend that I was in the arms of a loving parent.

Then one day came the best surprise of my whole young life; my maternal grandmother, Bobbie, came to live with us. O joy! Bobbie of the warm hugs and loving smiles was here to stay. And I didn't have to pretend anymore.

Grace happens.

Dot accepted her experience of grace with a deep sense of gratitude for all that she had, and seldom complained about what she had lost.

During one of our garden lunches the following summer, I commiserated with Dot about the limitations the surgery had imposed upon her.

"Feel free to complain," I suggested. "I know I would."

"Oh, nobody wants to hear that," replied Dot. "There are other things I would rather talk about."

Now, when I have my own moments to feel the need of a little "therapeutic whining," I think of Dot.

"Nobody wants to hear that."

Just when it seemed that the cancer might at last be in remission, a routine test indicated that the cancer had metastasized to Dot's liver. It was time to check with the experts at the Sloan-Kettering cancer center.

When the diagnostic evaluation was completed that spring, Dot met with the consulting specialist to discuss her prognosis. This was not a discussion. The doctor, who may well have been a diagnostic genius, badly needed some remedial work in empathic interaction. Somewhere along the line he had managed to confuse the title "M.D." with the grander title, "God, Jr."

After a terse description of the path the cancer was now taking, God, Jr. turned to leave the consulting room. But Dot wanted to know what she might expect in the coming months?

"Put it this way," the great doctor added, as his final summation, "Don't make any plans for Thanksgiving."

"I will make plans," Dot responded to his retreating back, ". . . and for Christmas and Easter, too." And that is exactly what she did. Grace happened.

Dot did not get to live forever. Nor will any of us. But she did get

several more very good years. Sometimes that is what healing really means. It is not forever. It is coming to a place of acceptance and peace, so that you can fully live the years that you are allotted.

Shortly after her diagnosis, Dot, ever the take-charge person, retired from her job as assistant director of a senior "citizens" home and became a resident there.

"Now," said Dot, with great relief, "I can continue to enjoy my family and friends. When the time comes that I can no longer take care of myself, I will not be a burden to anyone." The Dots of the world never do become burdens.

In the following few years, Dot got involved in church projects, traveled across the country, visited friends, and went on an island vacation with one of her sons. She truly lived until she died. That was her healing. Grace happens.

Early in our friendship, Dot once told me tearfully, that I had mentored her in the process of learning to value and care for herself. Now it is I who tearfully want to tell Dot that it was she who mentored me in learning how to die. And, in doing so, learning to live more fully.

The end of Dot's life was a slow, gentle, fading process. At the very end, when she was too weak to sit up, I would hold her hand and talk of the good times. When she was really tired, I gave her face massages with almond oil and we would be "be there."

We talked about our friendship and our time working together as therapists. I brought in the framed excerpt from Margery Williams' classic children's story, *The Velveteen Rabbit*, which had hung on the wall of our shared office space.

> *What is Real?*
> *"What is real?" asked the Rabbit*
> *one day, when they were lying*
> *side by side near the nursery*
> *fender . . .*
> *". . . does it mean having things*
> *that buzz inside you and a stick-out handle?"*

*"Real isn't how you are made,"*
*said the Skin Horse. "It's a thing that*
*happens to you. When a child loves*
*you for a long time, not just to*
*play with, but really loves you,*
*then you become Real. It doesn't*
*happen all at once.*
                          *You become.*

*"Generally, by the time you are*
*real, most of your hair has been*
*loved off, and your eyes drop out and*
*you get loose in the joints and*
*very shabby. But these things*
*don't matter at all, because when*
*you are Real, you can't be*
*ugly, except to people who*
*don't understand."*

"Good grief," I reminded her, "we were so real." We laughed together about all our earnest chats in the office Group Therapy room, where we always retired with our cookies and coffee when we were between clients.

"We are so open," we once declared. "We can always talk to each other about *anything.*" (This is what spending too much time with therapists can do to you.)

In all openness, I had suggested that Dot get a new hairstyle. "The way you wear it now, with your hair back and very short bangs above a high forehead, makes your head look like a hard-boiled egg."

"As long as we're being open," Dot responded, "You might consider talking less and emptying the garbage more." Now *that* was real.

Now, in Dot's final days, we could relive the good times we had shared. Sometimes, when Dot tired, I brought in poetry, mostly the verses that made us both smile, like Emily Dickinson.

*Hope is the thing with feathers*
*That perches in the soul—*
*And sings the tune without the words—*
*And never stops—at all—*

*And sweetest—in the Gale—is heard*
*and sore must be the storm—*
*That could abash the little Bird*
*That kept so many warm—*

*I've heard it in the chillest land—*
*And on the strangest sea—*
*Yet, never, in Eternity,*
*It asked a crumb—of me.*

The night she died I was able to tell her how loved she was, and then stroke her face in silence. When I was silent for too long, Dot's small voice seemed to come from far away . . . "Go on. I can hear you." But little by little she was slipping away.

I wanted to remain and walk together as far as we could go. But there was a loving family outside who needed to have their last moments alone with her. And I could feel Dot, peacefully and steadily, drifting toward the light.

"You are so loved," I whispered, laying my cheek against her face, "and you have lived your life with such grace."

Indeed, Grace happens.

CHAPTER 14

# A Time to
# Gather Stones Together

*Garbage becomes rose*
*Rose becomes compost—*
*Everything is in transformation.*
*Even permanence is impermanent.*
—Thich Nhat Hanh

mpermanence is not exactly a comforting thought, unless you are able to view impermanence itself as only a part of the ever-changing cycle of nature. Autumn is only sad if you see it as the dying off of the garden, rather than the dying back in preparation for the new season.

What you are witnessing is the first step of rebirth. The loss of the flowers means that they have now become compost from which will spring more flowers and new growth. Some, like the cleome, will already have dropped enough seeds to assure that by spring their progeny will be bursting forth. Often, they will be bursting, not only where you want them, but in many other places where you do not want them.

Our woodland garden is heavily planted with perennials and evergreen trees and shrubs, so autumn does not bring about the complete drab bareness that tends to appear in cottage gardens. Even so, each year I want to cling to the lushness of summer.

September, in my book, is back to school time. It is not the end of summer. Early October is the end of summer, when the leaves turn crimson and gold and the red maple is on fire.

When the first frost comes it devastates the beautiful, but wimpy, sensitive fern (onoclea sensibilis.) One day it is a lovely spreading fern growing in ever-widening clumps, each fern with its own unique undivided fronds. The next day following a frost the sensitive fern displays only tattered stalks, the devastated remains of sudden death. The impatiens fare no better. Overnight they have turned into a pulpy mass. *Now* it is autumn.

This is not death, I keep reminding myself. It is the beginning of new growth beneath the ground. As it is with our lives. Sometimes what seems to be a time of endless darkness, is a prelude to new light and new growth. Silent and invisible, the seeds of new life are already stirring.

> *You can count the number*
> *of apples on one tree, but*
> *you can never count the*
> *number of trees in one*
> *apple.*
> —Anonymous

As the leaves fall, once again it is time to assess the health needs of each tree. My friend, Michael, from the Good Earth Garden Center, comes over to begin again the arduous task of convincing me to let go of even one tree. He walks through the garden, looking about with the practiced eye of a landscape artist. I tag along behind, protesting each suggestion.

"This branch has got to go," says Michael, "and so does this one. Now, if you remove this old tree, it will open up the entire area and allow more sunlight to come through."

"No! No!" I plead. "This is a good tree."

But, it is not a good tree. It is an unhappy, dying tree that is both shading and crowding out the other smaller, but healthier trees and shrubs. I know this. But I planted this tree. So I am entitled to be protective of it. I also know that I am becoming an irrational tree hugger.

So, usually, I give in, again. Then I go into the house. I do not want to witness the demise of this once beautiful tree. When I return to the garden the tree is gone. In its place there is a shaft of sunlight highlighting the remaining trees and shrubs. They are pleased, for now they can spread out in comfort and reach for the sun.

Michael was right.

Our daily "garden tours" continue through the autumn months. Now there are different things to see. As the deciduous perennials go into hibernation the strength of the large tree trunks and the many evergreens appear as the dominant features. The "bones" of the garden become visible.

The lush plantings of epimedium, false nettle, pulmonaria and deciduous ferns, which have spent the summer months spilling over the edges of the walkways, have begun to die back.

Now, the many stones, which line the paths, are beginning to emerge. Light and dark, large and small, oval and round, they each have their own story. These are the "good time rocks."

The origin of these rocks goes back to the early days of the garden. Always, I have found rocks enchanting for their solidity and strength, and for the feeling of timeless energy they convey. Whenever we have had a pleasant experience I always bring home a "good time rock" to memorialize the occasion.

There have been smooth, palm-sized stones from outdoor country receptions, football-sized rocks from West Virginia, coral chunks from the islands, hefty irregular rocks from the Maine coast, Pennsylvania blue stone, and green-veined antiquities from Canada.

I have recently wondered if, with the advent of terrorism worries, I will one day be stopped at an airline luggage checkpoint. Will they confiscate my rocks for fear that they actually might be a primitive Neanderthal weapon?

In the beginning the rocks resided in piles on the patio and deck. As the piles grew I continued to marvel at all the good times we were having. Gradually, the rocks outgrew their location and found their way along the garden paths.

Now, family members began to bring their offerings. The children have brought shells and stones from the Jersey shore to South Carolina, from Alaska to the Philippines. Scattered throughout the garden, the stones are no longer labeled as to their origin. They just form a great merged entity, like some giant collective unconscious of energy.

The rock-lined paths have such a strength and beauty of their own that in recent years I have added additional stones from a local quarry to carry the paths to completion.

My last trip to the quarry was after the surgery which followed a serious knee injury. Before that experience I had never noticed that a quarry is a really large, dusty, very difficult place in which to maneuver, even if you have *two* good legs.

Upon entering the quarry, the driver positions his vehicle on a large ramp, where it will be weighed before and after loading the stones. I say "he" because most of the drivers are large, burly men in large burly trucks, that have manly things written on the sides. I weigh 106 pounds and drive a little, gray, sissy car. So when we drive into the rock-loading areas I rarely win the right-of-way disputes.

Once in the loading area, the drivers back their big trucks up to the rock piles and begin scooping up rocks by the truckload. That is, unless I just happen to slide in ahead of them in my little sissy car. Then the big trucks sit there, roaring their engines while their drivers say ugly things.

On my last trip I parked my little car next to a choice pile of rocks and stumbled out, leaning heavily on my cane. Walking over rocks while using a cane is no easy task. Carrying the stones back, one stone at a time, using only my free arm was no picnic, either. But it was worth it to me. The truck drivers' sentiments were a bit different.

The waiting drivers did not exactly suffer in silence. It would serve no purpose to repeat their remarks. However, I was as stubborn as they were rude. So I continued to select my beauties, one stone at a time, until the back of the car was dragging to the ground. All the while the men fumed and raced their truck engines.

Since then, after destroying the suspension on my car and re-arranging a few discs in my back, I have reluctantly come to the realization that if I am to get more rocks I will need to subcontract a strong back.

Enter Jason, the resident aesthetic at the garden center, who instantly understood that getting a stone didn't mean any stone. It meant just the right stone. We could spend an endless amount of time discussing the exact place each stone should go, and what the size and "feel" of that stone should be.

Then, like a Japanese stone broker, Jason would visit the quarry and search out the most beautiful lichen-covered stones that called out to be brought to this garden. You either understand these things, or you don't. Jason did. When he returned with the stones we would repeat the process all over again, deciding exactly which stone was right for each spot.

In just this way, this little place has been touched by so many who have entered the garden and left a piece of themselves in the spirit of this sacred space.

The rock-strewn garden path leads directly to the compost pile. Unless, of course, you detour past the ICU. The Intensive Care Unit resides on a semi-shady hill opposite the compost pile.

This is the last chance home for plants that are tired, sickly, or in the final stages of deterioration . In other words, plants that any sensible gardener would have trashed long ago. I always like to give them one more chance to make it.

So, to the hill they go. Newly planted in a nice compost filled hole, the dying plants are watered and coddled. Here, they have a spacious environment to relax and reflect on their options. It is possible that because the plants now face the compost pile they are aware of the other option. This could be a powerful motivating factor.

So many of these almost throwaways are now thriving that the ICU periodically has to be cleared out. The survivors are returned to choicer spots in the garden. Perhaps, just like people, the seemingly hopeless plants can make it if they can just get enough support and nurture.

Our compost pile is actually a rather fancy affair. It is constructed of 4 x 4s widely spaced, with wire hardware cloth between the boards to allow for the entry of air without the loss of compost. Into the pile goes everything that once lived, excluding animal and dairy products. Essentially, compost is just deteriorating organic matter.

They don't call the compost "black gold" for nothing. It is filled with nutrients and enriches any plant that is the lucky beneficiary. Not only is this an ecologically sound way to avoid filling our landfills with garbage and garden debris, even more important, it is a way to re-create the process of growth that nature provides in the natural woodland.

The compost pile is assembled like a giant cake with brown and green layers. The bottom of the pile is lined with small sticks and branches that will help to provide a little air circulation beneath the pile. Next comes a generous helping of dirt. For the green layer, grass cuttings, dying plants and vegetables will compost nicely. This is followed with a little more dirt, rotting leaves and twigs.

You can go on and on with this formula. Nature will then do the rest of the work for you. There is something so comforting about being a part of this.

Composting, as with all of life in the garden, becomes for me a way of experiencing myself as a piece of the eternal cycle of the life process. The poet, Joyce Fossen speaks to those feelings.

> *Do not stand at my grave and weep*
> *I am not there. I do not sleep.*
>
> *I am a thousand winds that blow*
> *I am the diamond glint on snow.*
>
> *I am the sunlight on ripened grain.*
> *I am the gentle autumn rain.*
>
> *When you wake in the morning hush*
> *I am the swift, uplifting rush*
> *of quiet birds in circling flight.*
> *I am the soft starlight at night.*
>
> *Do not stand at my grave and weep*
> *I am not there. I do not sleep."*
> —Joyce Possen

To me it simply boils down to:

*Do not stand at my grave and weep.*
*My soul lives on. I do not sleep.*

CHAPTER 15

# A Time
# to Die

*With all your science, can
you tell how it is, and where
it is, that light comes into
the soul?*
—Henry David Thoreau

 utumn is the time of putting the garden to bed in preparation for the next season of growth. It is also a bittersweet time for me for it has been a time of losses in my own life. In a few short years I lost Alta and Dot, my very dear friends, and both of my parents. All in the Autumn of the year.

My mother's death came after several years of failing health. It was not unexpected. She died in a quiet, gentle way, much the same way she had lived. Nonetheless, dealing with the death of a mother is never easy. She is the one who brought you into this world, a connection that lasts a lifetime.

Your mother is the person at whose feet you lay your trophies. She is the one to whom you can brag a little. The one you can tell when life just isn't fair. The one to whom you call and say, "Guess What, Mom?"

Now it is *my* son and daughter who call and say, "Guess What, Mom?" And my grandsons, Brian and Patrick, who call and say, "Guess What, Allie?" And, of course, Michelle, who will call to report if she is "not being

129

treated fairly." I don't worry too much about that. Generally, it is only a child who has been brought up knowing that love and fairness count, who feels free enough to comment on the subject.

So, I know what it means to be truly blessed.

It was harder when my father died. The man who could never acknowledge his own mortality had lived a very long and active life. At the end his heart just gave out.

"*If* I die, my father announced the summer before his death, "I want you to do the same kind of eulogy for me that you did for your mother."

"Yes-s," I promised, hesitantly, wondering how I could do this. The eulogy for my mother had focused on her kind, gentle nature. My father had not been a kind and gentle person.

During my father's last days I was experiencing a difficult recovery from a shattered knee. In those gray November days I sat in a wheelchair and looked out over the garden. Some of the tree branches were bare and dry leaves littered the patio, but it was still beautiful.

I studied the barren trees and the sturdy evergreens behind them and struggled with how I would have the strength to be there for my father at the end.

Once again the garden offered me a place of serenity where I could struggle with the conflicting feelings about my father's coming death. Or, if he lived a bit longer, how I would deal with his repeated suggestion that he leave his retirement community and come to live with us. The possibility of that occurring was too painful to contemplate.

It seemed more likely that my father would die. I did not want to wish that on him. How, I wondered, could I say goodbye to my father; provide him with support and compassion, and still remain true to myself?

Gradually, I became aware that I needed just to offer it up. My father's death was in God's hands, not mine. And, once again, I realized that this is one of the ways God speaks—when I take the time to listen.

For a long time I pondered over how best to fulfill my father's request

to write the eulogy that he wanted and still remain honest. My mind wandered back through the memories of my childhood years.

I grew up a long way from Sunny Brook Farm. Denying that would not be an honest eulogy. As I have witnessed many times in my own therapeutic practice, caring about one's children and treating them badly are not always mutually exclusive categories. This can be especially true of an adult who remains one of God's broken children, long after his own sad childhood is over.

But to focus on the unhappiness would be to lose the valuable memories of the good times. And there *were* good times, too.

It was the garden that rescued me. I remember the sun-drenched cosmos of my childhood. When my father tended those flowers, he seemed more like the kinder, gentler person that I longed for him to be. In a way, he was the one who started me on the garden path.

It was walking down that garden path in the memory of my childhood that reminded me of my long ago jungle gym.

How could I forget the autumn of the jungle gym? That was the year I was in sixth grade. It was not my best year. That's how I could forget it.

This was the year when most of the girls in my class were beginning to acquire a shape. Not me. I looked the same, coming and going. It was my destiny to be a midget, I decided. And not a midget who was just a short person. I would be a midget who always looked as if she were just entering kindergarten.

This was the year that my arch rival, Barbara, strutted through the locker room wearing her new bra. Just strutting was not enough. She had to point out all the lace trimming and say, "Ohh-h, it's so comfortable."

I pretended not to notice. That was easy because I was hunkered down behind the locker door in my Fruit of the Loom undershirt. I wanted to smack her. I wanted to *be* her.

"Be thankful that you look so young," consoled my mother. "When you are thirty, you'll be glad."

"Yeah, right," I smiled. "When I'm thirty, I'll be too old to care."

"What did my mother know, anyway?" I thought. This is the woman who takes me to the Hot Shoppes and instructs the waitress to give me the children's menu. Doesn't she know that it is embarrassing enough to be

seen in the Hot Shoppes with your parents? To be in sixth grade and be seen ordering the Humpty Dumpty Platter could mean social ruin.

For the past year I had been secretly pining for the affection of Googy Carr. Googy had yet to pine for any female, let alone one who was wearing Fruit of the Loom.

Then came the wonderful season of the jungle gym. One weekend, my father transformed our entire backyard into a child's fantasy of swings, trapezes, hanging rings and walking ladders, all of which he crafted himself. It was a child's dream come true. For the rest of the year, I was the Queen of the Jungle Gym.

The appearance of the jungle gym was soon followed by the appearance of Googy Carr. I loved Googy. Googy loved the trapeze. That was good enough for me. Googy was soon followed by Clarence, who dropped by every day after school, as soon as he could run home and change into his Superman suit.

Life was good. Okay, so I still didn't need a bra. But who needs a bra when they are Queen of the Jungle Gym?

Eat your heart out, Barbara.

That was the gift of the garden. I could remember the man of the golden cosmos. The man who cared enough to build a jungle gym. The man who might have been like that more often if his own life had been less painful.

I will never forget finding an old photograph of my father . . . to me it looked like who he was meant to be: a little, spindly, tow-headed tyke with sparkling eyes and neatly parted yellow hair. He had perched on a carved chair and exuded all the vulnerability and bright promise of my own children and grandchildren.

But there were not any more happy pictures to be found. I can only piece together the painful experiences which that little boy later endured, experiences that took the trusting light out of those eyes. And the pain that, in his darker side, he ultimately passed on to his family.

When the human spirit is too battered, we all respond differently to that early bruising. Some survive and fly. Some are shattered and some become a rock.

I think of the lyrics to Simon and Garfunkel's "I Am a Rock."

My father survived as a rock who felt no pain. And, because he could not feel his own pain, he could not comprehend the pain in others. This was a defense for which he paid dearly.

Always he walked the road alone. The boy who had been let down so badly, could not trust again. Pop used to say, "I don't have any friends. I don't need any."

The island that was my father could not even grasp his own loneliness. I think that people who wish vengeance on others whose behavior is unacceptable, might not need that vengeance so much if they realized that the person they hate is already paying a high price, whether or not they realize it. If Hell is just as simple as separation from God, then perhaps for some, where Hell begins is on earth.

Remembering the "island that never cried" has helped me to forgive my father. So has offering it up. Prayer, if you will. Prayer doesn't change the situation. It changes me. Like the turn of a kaleidoscope, the same pieces make a different picture.

Forgiveness follows. It doesn't mean that bad behavior is okay. It doesn't mean that you haven't experienced anger along with the pain. It just means releasing the feelings because you have a better sense of the bigger picture.

In his last years, I visited my father regularly. But, because I had so frequently feared him as a child, I could not touch him as an adult. I know that he felt this distance. When he became ill, I had planned that, as soon as my leg healed and I could walk again, I would go to the Health Care Center and try to reach out and comfort him.

I knew how much my father feared death. And I thought that I would take his hand and walk with him as far as I could go, so that he would not die alone.

But we do not always get to draw our own map. On a gray Friday morning my father, who so feared pain and death, was granted a slip into unconsciousness and a gentle, quiet death.

When the call came that my father was dying, it was sooner than we had expected. Because I was alone at home in a wheelchair and unable to drive, I could only wait frantically for a ride which did not come in time. I did not get there for his last moments. It happened too fast. So I could not take his hand for that final trip.

Later, my friend, Pat, comforted me. "Alice," she said, "when you give his eulogy, that is when you will take his hand." And that is what happened. I did get to give my father his eulogy and it came from the heart.

It was with great sadness that I said goodbye to my father. Not just for what was, but for what might have been. I can accept now that sometimes the wounded spirit does not heal. We do not always know who will fly— and who will break.

At last I could truly say, "Pop, I forgive you. And I forgive myself for not being able to go beyond the hurt child within me to the broken child in you."

And so the garden helped me to remember the man who planted a thousand cosmos, and to forgive the man who paid such a high price for his anger. May God be kind to my father, and may he find his garden in the next life.

CHAPTER 16

# *A Time to Keep*

As long as the earth endures,
Seedtime and harvest, cold and
heat, summer and winter, day
and night, shall not cease.
—Genesis 8:22

s autumn folds into winter the days grow colder, and the frosts of autumn give way to the winter's chill and freezing rain and snow. Even then, the "garden tour" goes on. But now the ice tea has been replaced with steaming cups of coffee.

The "bones" of the garden have moved from mere visibility to prominence. The tall, stately pines, spruces and hollies seem darker, richer and greener. The "good time rocks" lining the pathways get to show off their own charms. Solid and strong, in many shapes and shades of grays and browns, each stone stands unique in its own form and markings. Yet, each has some similarity to the others, much like members of a large, extended family.

Despite the cold, the paths continue to invite the viewer to follow them to yet another beautiful space. The azaleas and rhododendrons remain green and thick. But the poor rhododendron goes into panic when the really deep freeze settles in. Every single, once broad, leaf has now turned into a skinny leaf, as it curls tightly around itself to escape the chill. The unhappy shrub now resembles a large, woody bush covered with hundreds of hanging cigars.

*Coreopsis*

The holly and nandina shrubs shine with brilliant, red berries, which delight us, as well as the birds. These berries will provide their winter snacks. All along the paths we stop to admire the survivor plants. The hellebores and the Christmas ferns carry on bravely, although the Christmas fern is now becoming a bit tatty around the edges.

The pachysandra and periwinkle ground covers remain as stalwarts of the garden. The indestructible pachysandra is the thicker and stronger of the two. The liriope continues to form a thick mat. However, soon enough this mat will be diminished when the rabbits decide to make this patch their winter salad bar.

This time the rabbit is our helper. He has freed us from the task of cutting back all the liriope plants, as recommended by the gardening experts, who explain that this will produce a stronger plant in the spring. They are right. By spring the rabbits have moved on to decimate greener pastures, leaving behind the liriope, which returns thicker than ever.

The deciduous perennials have long since surrendered their greenery to the chill of winter. All that remains are the dead, brown stalks. This no longer saddens me, for I am now acutely aware that below the earth they are only sleeping. Even as their visible remains shrivel, they are spreading out their roots, preparing for new growth.

Now that I have a sense of this I no longer whine about the cold. Well, not so much, anyway. Although I would never go so far as Andrew Wyeth and say that I actually prefer winter.

By early spring the bulbs and plants will begin resurrecting themselves, bursting forth with new life, and proving yet again that sacred space isn't just in the sanctuary.

The garden itself has become a metaphor for our own lives. Sometimes, in the therapy process, I have utilized this metaphor with clients

who are dealing with pain and loss in their lives. They, too, feel "dead above the ground" and struggle to find the courage to risk again, or to believe in tomorrow.

This is the same message so beautifully expressed by Amanda McBroom in the lyrics of her song, "The Rose." For one client, a strong woman, who had experienced so much pain for so long that she questioned the wisdom of continuing to hope, this simple song spoke to her in a very powerful way. The feelings that surfaced became a starting point for some meaningful discussions about her own spiritual beliefs and life decisions.

While we are waiting for spring to become the rose, and the earth is still rigid with the frost, the rabbits continue to feast on the liriope, and the red fox continues to feast on the rabbits. There is a certain flow and harmony to this pattern unless, of course, you happen to be on the evening menu.

The birds provide a parade of color and activity as they fly about, unmolested, all winter. They may be cold, but they are happy. The wicked cat is now confined indoors. "Boots," the cat, has now been supplanted by "Timothy," who has an equally bad attitude toward creatures that are smaller than himself. Like "Boots," he also continues to curry my favor. It always works. But Timothy does not like the damp chill of winter and is willing now to settle for central heat and Tender Vittles.

As gardeners we consider it to be our responsibility to provide food and sanctuary for the birds during the winter months. Consequently, our plantings include many berries for the birds, as well as trees and shrubs for shelter. The largest pond sports a heating ring and a small, raised mini-pond which spills over into the main body of water. So the birds are treated to lukewarm bathing and drinking year round.

The moderate income housing unit, and the other assorted bird houses, are always there for the birds to take shelter in when the weather is extremely cold. As the landlord, I expect them to provide at least their own upkeep. I am now resigned to the fact that the birds have a very bad track

record in this area. So, in the early spring, I pour pitchers of hot water through each house to clean out the bird lice and any other disgusting things that may be lurking there.

It is a joy to watch the birds as they sing and fly about, shouting insults at each other. The blue jays are among the most beautiful, in spite of their incessant bad-mouth squawking and complaining. The big mouth catbird can match them for noise, but with his mousy feathers he is no competition in the arena of beauty. The cardinal is, of course, my favorite. His vivid crimson feathers add sparkle to the winter scene and, unlike the beautiful blue jay, his manners are impeccable.

I can now recognize the obvious birds like robins, bluebirds, wood-peckers, crows, wrens and finches. The rest of the bird kingdom are rel-egated to the status of brown guy, gray guy, and yellow guy. Later, I shall learn all their proper names, and even own my very own binoculars.

Then I will be able to sound knowledgeable and say things like: "Oh, I say, I do believe that is an indigo bunting!" But that is going to have to wait until I have mastered the cello, learned to speak Spanish, and have acquired some minimal sense of what is going on with my computer.

Because the birds need high energy and high fat foods like suet, fruits, seeds and nuts, we have stopped leaving bread crumbs in the bird feeders. Bread, for birds, is the nutritional equivalent of fast food. A bird stuffed with bread is going to be just that — stuffed. But he will be without the necessary fuel to withstand the cold winter. Birds need bread like humans need Burger King.

Instead, we have provided peanut butter treats. No treat recipe is necessary. A glob of peanut butter smeared on the bird feeder, a stump, or a tree trunk is enormously attractive to birds and highly nutritious as well.

The squirrels concur with this opinion and race to beat out the birds for any available treat. I quite like the squirrels. They are aggressively funny. They may be greedy, but they never harm the birds. I have chosen not to fight the eternal losing battle my fellow gardeners wage to keep the squirrels out of the bird feeders. I prefer to define them as an additional resident of the woodland that I am choosing to feed.

Try this mantra: The squirrel is my friend, he is *not* just a bushy-tailed rodent." This way, when you patrol the feeders for intruders, you can occasionally exclaim: "Oh, look! The birds have gotten in the squirrel feeder again."

During these cold months, Wilma and her extended raccoon family are, as to be expected, up to no good. Looking like a crowd of bandit-faced pandas, these trouble makers have started behaving like a group of rowdy adolescents. The garbage is strewn about, and the pond is looted.

Instead of going peacefully to their den under the deck, they thump up to the flat roof over our bedroom. I do not even want to know how they got there. In the middle of the night their thumping can be heard coming from above the ceiling over our head.

Soon the scurrying of many little feet can be heard. Now comes: Thump! Thump! Thump! Scurry, Scurry, Scurry, Thump! Thump! Thump! They are probably playing volleyball with the remnants of our garbage.

I laugh, but Stan is not amused. He opens the window and bellows some moderately uncivilized suggestions to the volleyball team. About this time I am wondering if the neighbors are beginning to suspect that the Millers are having some serious problems themselves.

Silence descends. Soon timorous, little feet tiptoe across the roof. Then all is silent again. In a few minutes there is a thumping on the deck below. We look out the window just in time to see four bushy, gray butts waddling off into the dark. This is too funny.

In the morning when I check the garbage area, it is just as Stan predicted, a disaster. Now, I am the one not laughing. That is because I am considering making a Wilma stew.

In spite of all this, I had always assumed that annoyances aside, the story of Wilma, her three sons, and her extended family, would just be an ongoing saga. But this story does not have a happy ending. One recent winter night when Stan went to fill the trash can, he heard a loud crashing noise and arrived to discover Wilma, who was by now the size of a grossly overweight cocker spaniel, emerging from what she considered to be *her* garbage.

Stan, as he had in past encounters, picked up the broom handle and banged it loudly on the wall. This was Wilma's cue to make a speedy departure. But, this time Wilma reared up, stood her ground, and then approached to take him on. This was not an encounter that Stan wanted to experience. So it was Stan who made the speedy departure. But, from then on, Wilma's days were numbered.

With the help of a humane trapping service Wilma succumbed to the lure of an open sardine can placed in a steel mesh trap. I could hardly bear to see her confined in that small space. But, when she looked at me with angry beady eyes, I was suddenly very glad that she was on the inside and I was on the outside.

Supposedly, Wilma would be re-located to a new and distant woodland setting. I have since suspected that the "far away setting" was a euphemism for the great raccoon woodland in the sky. And, sadder still, what will become of her three sons— Manny, Moe, and Jack?

While the animals are braving the chill of winter, the annual ritual of Christmas is about to begin. How symbolic it is that in a dark month of Winter, we pause to celebrate the light of Christmas.

In the gospel of Luke, the Christmas Story unfolds with a whole mess of angels and hallelujas. But the gospel according to John skips all the fanfare and cuts right to the chase.

> *—And the Word became flesh*
> *and dwelt among us, full of grace*
> *and truth—for the law was*
> *given through Moses; grace and*
> *truth came through Jesus Christ.*
> —John 14, 18

It seems pretty simple, really. No one has ever seen God. Once, long ago, he was seen through Jesus and lived as a man with all the feelings of joy, love, sadness and anger. But, mostly, the love. With His life he demonstrated the love of God. That *is* the Christmas Story. The word was made flesh and dwelt among us. God is Love.

This is what the Church is about—telling the story.

"Telling the story" was succinctly summed up by a sermon in which Roy recounted a story told by Martin Buber, the Jewish philosopher and theologian. This was his grandfather's holy story.

Dr. Buber's grandfather was very old and frail. Crippled up and barely able to move, the old man made a pilgrimage to visit the dancing holy man. No ordinary holy man, this man danced as he talked.

Upon his return home, Dr. Buber's grandfather wanted to share with his family his deeply moving experience with the dancing holy man. As the old man told his story he began to demonstrate the movements of the holy man. Soon he was dancing himself. Gradually, as he danced, he became aware that he was no longer crippled.

What a wonderful tale. The story itself becomes a metaphor for bearing witness. For the witness himself was made whole by the telling of the story. When you tell the story you become, in doing so, like the one whose story you tell.

Telling the story is partly about "feeling" the story. Christmas, then, is about once again feeling that this is a time of new birth.

One "silent night" in December I experienced that with my children. It had been preceded by one of those glistening, bright winter days that remind you that winter can bring its own magic.

All afternoon the sun sparkled in glittery diamonds on a fresh carpet of snow. All around, the neighborhood children were rolling in the drifts, pulling their sleds over the crusted snow, and just laughing at the joy of it all. Surely, I thought, there is nothing so beautiful as this.

But there is. When the snow falls silently in the middle of the night and the whole world turns silver and still, *that* is even more beautiful. That is the way is was on that night of snow angels.

It had been a cold, crisp winter night when I awoke at 3 a.m. The snow was falling in heavy, fat flakes on the streets and lawns that were already wearing a blanket of white. I watched the flakes gleam in the glow of the street lights. It was so beautiful, it could shatter your heart. I *had* to be out there.

Sometimes in life you just need to leap into an experience when the moment arrives, while it is still there. I wanted my children to know that feeling. Tara and Kevin, still in the early years of elementary school, were sound asleep in preparation for their morning classes. But some experiences in life are worth the price of being a little tired the next day.

The children were delighted to be awakened for an adventure. We quietly donned our snowsuits, scarves, boots and mittens and tiptoed to the front door. By now Moses, our bumbling, 150-pound Saint Bernhard, was up and ready for his own adventure.

We walked out into a silent, white world. On a snowy midweek, middle-of-the-night, suburbia was in a deep, dark sleep. All around was nothing but snow and stillness. We were the only people in the world. It felt like the dawn of creation. It felt sacred.

"It feels like I am the deer inside my paperweight," whispered Kevin. He had recently gotten one of those round glass ball paperweights which contained a small deer statue inside the globe. When turned upside down, the globe released a flood of white flakes that completely engulfed the deer. Now, Kevin was enchanted that he, like the deer, could feel the magic.

"Oh," exclaimed Tara, in awe. Whenever completely taken over with an experience, Tara always responded with a series of soft "oh-h-hs." At Christmas I always knew I had picked the right present when Tara emitted one of her breathy "oh-h-hs." They were far more eloquent than mere words.

The silence enfolded us. You could barely hear the gentle touch of the new snow as it alighted on the white carpet. It was like pieces of velvet gently coming together. The kids were awed. No need for words now.

Moses was bred for this kind of weather. Soon his white, brown and black fur became a fluffy, white coat. He plowed through the drifts in ecstasy. I think Moses was hoping for someone to rescue. Finally, he realized that that was not going to happen because, for right now, for this very moment, we were the only people (and dog) in the whole world.

The four of us walked and walked throughout the silent neighborhood. The world was ours. We tried catching snowflakes on our upturned faces and tongues. Then we tried running, but the snow was too deep. Instead, we bounced along making hoppy movements up and down

through the drifts. Moses thought this was a splendid idea and joined us. He was much better at it than any of us.

Then, as a gift to the neighbors, we each laid flat on everyone's front lawn and swung our arms back and forth to make the impressions of snow angels. By morning the angel outlines would be filled with the falling snow. But, for us, the snow angels will always remain.

Now my children are adults and, when it snows, they need to go out and clean off their cars so they can get to work on time. But they have never forgotten the night of the snow angels. And neither have I.

# CHAPTER 17

# A Time
# to Be Born — Anew

*Morning has broken like the first morning,*
*Blackbird has spoken like the first bird.*
*Praise for the singing! Praise for the morning!*
*Praise for them springing fresh from the word!*
—Eleanor Farjeon, 1931

 t is always the "first morning" in the garden. But, never is that more gloriously true than in the springtime. Already the helleborous have been nodding their little pink and white heads. Everywhere the forsythia have burst forth with masses of golden blooms, and the ground is dotted with purple and yellow crocus.

Edna St. Vincent Millay was right. "April comes in like an idiot, babbling and strewing flowers." She could have been writing about me. Every year when the season's first warm breath of air arrives I, too, am babbling about and strewing flowers. The "idiot" part of that analogy we can overlook.

I prefer the term "selective amnesia." Every spring my convenient amnesia allows me, once again, to forget that in Maryland the first warm sunny days are invariably followed by the random last gasps of winter. Then, with little warning, the sun is replaced with dark, ominous clouds and a hard, killing frost.

Every year when the garden center puts out those brave little flats of brightly colored annuals I am the first in line to fill my little wagon. This

year, I tell myself, it is going to be warm and
beautiful all season. I can hardly wait to plant
the flowers.

And so the rites of spring begin. On goes
my dolphin hat and out I go to perform, yet
again, the annual spring ritual of putting the
geraniums out to die.

Always there are pots of cheerful red and
white and pink geraniums on my porch and
patio, and gracing the edges of the herb beds. And always, there are the
casualties who did not get brought inside the night of the freezing rain.

There is a reason for this perpetual disaster. These beautiful, brilliant
pink and red geraniums are not really geraniums. They are pelargoniums,
a tender perennial flower, native to South Africa. In the colder North
American climate the pelargoniums have become an annual. The "true"
geraniums are perennials that thrive in North America and grow in the
filtered sun or the light shade of a woodland garden. The geraniums are
most often seen in subtle shades of pink and blue. For me, no woodland
garden would be complete without a few Johnson Blue geraniums spreading along the pathways.

The pelargoniums, which I, and every nursery in town, continue to
call geraniums, are considered by purists to be quite gaudy and common.
I like gaudy and common. They are cheerful and bright and thrive in
almost any soil, boldly surviving the occasional drought. In Switzerland
the window boxes abound with masses of these pink and red pompoms
which bloom in profusion through the spring and summer months. Once
seeing them in full bloom there, I would never be without them in my
own garden.

Although I know that these geraniums are annuals, they make me so
happy I just can't resist putting them out early anyway. 'Who knows?' I
say every spring. This could be the start of the first year of the completely
mild, early spring. All too often, this is the night of the arctic blast.

There is a message in here somewhere, and I don't want to hear it.
But, what can you expect from someone whose hero is Don Quixote, and
"Dream the Impossible Dream."

Spring does this to me. It is such a joyous season. A time to just let loose . . . a time to feel beneficent toward everyone. Thoreau understood this.

As every season seems best to us in its turn, so the coming in of spring is like the creation of Cosmos out of Chaos and the realization of the Golden Age . . .

> A single gentle rain makes the grass many shades greener. So our prospects brighten on the influx of better thoughts. We should be blessed if we lived in the present always, and took advantage of every accident that befell us, like the grass which confesses the influence of the slightest dew that falls on it; and did not spend our time in atoning for the neglect of past opportunities, which we call doing our duty. We loiter in winter while it is already spring. In a pleasant spring morning all men's sins are forgiven. Such a day is a truce to vice. While such a sun holds out to burn, the vilest sinner may return. Through our own recovered innocence we discern the innocence of our neighbors. You may have known your neighbor yesterday for a thief, a drunkard, or a sensualist, and merely pitied or despised him, and despaired of the word; but the sun shines bright and warm this spring morning, re-creating the world, and you meet him at some serene work, and see how his exhausted and debauched veins expand with still joy and bless the new day, feel the spring influence with the innocence of infancy, and all his faults are forgotten.
> —Henry David Thoreau

Like Thoreau's creation of cosmos, out of the chaos and the realization of the "Golden Age" when Spring arrives, I, too am outside checking on my own cosmos out of the chaos.

So, when I am not busy killing the geraniums, I am walking down the garden paths enjoying the multiple plantings of daffodils sprinkled randomly among the trees. Some even peek from beneath the shrubs, looking for all the world as if they had done this all by themselves. They have not.

Every summer I pounce on the advance fall planting catalog from my

*Daffodil*

old standby, the White Flower Farm. After pouring over eye popping displays of multi-colored daffodils, I usually resort to my old favorite order, the ultimate daffodil purchase, called "The Works."

The collection arrives at planting time in a big, stout cardboard carton containing 100 bulbs of at least 30 different varieties. Each variety blooms at a different time, and each propagates in its own time, to add to the appearance of a naturalized woodland. They come in all sizes, and the colors range from the palest white through warm cream, and from clear yellow to a deep, rich gold. Each year there are more new surprises as these beautiful symbols of spring burst forth into bloom.

When the first chill days of autumn arrive, we always set out half of the new bulbs in random spots throughout the garden. The remaining bulbs I put in groups of three or four to a plastic grower's pot filled with soil from the compost pile. The pots are then tucked in mulch filled whiskey half-barrels and covered with an additional thick topping of mulch. There they await the end of another cold winter.

By the end of winter, I am daily peeling off the top layers of mulch, to peer in, much like an anxious mother checking on her babies. As the daffodils begin to sprout I bring them into the house to enjoy. The late sprouting plants are added to the collection of patio pots. Then, when spring is in full swing, I can see clearly the gaps in the garden where the new bulbs can be planted in the best possible "random" location.

Some of the seemingly random patches of daffodils along the paths and among the trees are the result of a considerable amount of unsolicited help from the squirrels. These bushy tailed rodents lurk in the trees, spying on the unsuspecting gardeners as they carefully plant their bulbs for the following spring.

In the dark of the night, the squirrels descend and loot the new plantings for their own private munch-fest. The leftovers they dig in se-

cret hiding places as a stash for the coming months. Of course, the squirrels never put the leftover bulbs back where they got them. In the morning, the gardeners awake to discover the freshly dug piles of earth and the small craters that once housed the new bulbs.

There is no point in moaning about it. This is as inevitable as the wind and the rain and the snow. Besides, the squirrels always miss more than they steal. Also, there is an unexpected bonus. Many of these bushy tailed looters appear to be suffering from a rodent form of Alzheimer's disease. By the time spring arrives they have long since forgotten where they have buried their treasures. The gardener will then be treated to an unexpected array of bulbs, popping up in the most unlikely places.

It is always amazing to see how these squirrel-propagated bulbs settle in and naturalize all by themselves. This is in spite of the fact that the squirrel has never bothered to read the planting instructions. How does he know that the bulb must be placed with the root end down, spaced properly, and planted at the correct depth?

Yet, the squirrels' offerings appear to flourish as well as mine. Next year I plan to just throw all the new bulbs around the garden and let the squirrels do *all* the planting.

But, with or without the squirrel's "help," there is much to be done in the spring garden. Debris from the winter must be cleared up and compost and mulch laid down. The beautiful garden, spiritual place that it may be, does not happen all by itself. Rudyard Kipling was quick to point this out in his poem, "Glory of the Garden."

> *Our England is a garden that is full of stately views,*
> *Of borders, beds and shrubberies and lawns and avenues,*
> *With statues on the terraces and peacocks strutting by;*
> *But the glory of the Garden lies in more than meets the eye.*
>
> *The Glory of the Garden it abideth not in words.*
> *Our England is a garden, and such gardens are not made*
> *By singing: "oh, how beautiful!" and sitting in the shade,*
> *While better men than we go out and start their working lives*
> *At grubbing weeds from gravel paths with broken dinner knives.*

*Then seek your job with thankfulness and work till further orders.*
*If it's only netting strawberries or killing slugs on borders;*
*And when your back stops aching and your hands begin to harden,*
*You will find yourself a partner in the glory of the Garden.*

*Oh, Adam was a gardener, and God who made him sees*
*That half a proper gardener's work is done upon his knees,*
*So when your work is finished, you can wash your hands and pray*
*For the Glory of the Garden it shall never pass away!*

And when the glory of the daffodils begins to pass away, the kwanzan cherry tree, planted in the center of the deck, moves from bud to full bloom in an explosion of pale pink blossoms. Soon the entire garden is blazing with the rich dazzling crimsons, pinks and whites of the azaleas. Spring is full upon us.

Every spring brings new surprises. The under-story plantings of shrubs, wildflowers and ferns continue to expand, and the ground cover plants cannot wait to propagate themselves. With every passing season they become even more lush.

The young trees from our early springs have now matured. Their formerly misshapen lower branches have long since been elevated. In one corner, the once sun-dappled, lightly shaded area has now matured into a heavily shaded woodland, thick with ferns. In the summer months it is cool and serene. This is the new place of sanctuary for the hammock.

In another area, the loss of a large tree has suddenly converted a deeply shaded spot into a sunny patch. Now, the plum tip Nandina grows thick and lush and the Euphorbia around it has begun to spread with the gift of added light. Later in the season the Queen Anne's Lace and the Black-eyed Susans will find the sunlight and decide to stay and raise a few families of their own.

So, even as the garden continues to mature, it also continues to grow. While some parts are, of necessity, dying back, other parts are putting out fresh growth. Something new is always happening.

To me, this is nature's message for our own lives. If we accept an "old-

young" young paradigm, then we choose to view our life as a series of diminishing choices. But, when we use the "old-new" paradigm, the choices are endless.

That works for me. I will never be young again, but that is okay. I am a much nicer person now, and I always have the option of being "new." There is no need to worry about forgetting this option. For spring returns every year to remind us all over again. That is what re-birth is all about.

It is in this spirit of new beginnings that I am now learning to play the cello. For me, this has been a giant leap into the dark. In my family of origin, music was not important, at least, "not for girls." It was a world I could never enter.

Secretly, I yearned to have this experience. To become a cellist was, for me, the ultimate fantasy. No other instrument can match the mellow, rich tones of the cello, not in my book. But, the acute awareness that I lack any musical knowledge, or any basic skills, has always held me back. "Stringed instruments are for people with real talent." I got the message.

"Get a recorder," suggested a friend, on hearing my impossible dream. "The cello is one of the more difficult instruments to learn to play."

"I don't want a recorder," I pouted. So the impossible dream was shelved. It became another wonderful idea to pursue in the "future."

It was my family who reminded me that "the future is now." This past Christmas, in what was one of the most loving gifts I could ever receive, there was a big, beautiful cello— with my name on it! What, I wondered tearfully, could be more beautiful than having a family who embraces your dream?

Those grateful feelings brought to mind the words sung at Passover, "It would have been enough . . ." It was enough, at first. But, after I finished being overwhelmed, I realized that I had no idea of how to play the cello.

And then I found Louis Roberts. A top rate cello teacher, Louis was just who I needed. But, would he want me? I couldn't read music, I was temporarily tone deaf, when singing, I had a range of three notes. And I didn't even know which three they were. .

"I'll never be one of your better students," I warned Louis, "but I will

be the one who tries the hardest. I know I have music inside. I need you to help me get it out." And that is just what he is doing.

All of his students love Louis, I am quite sure. I know I do. Always, he is so patient and kind. He didn't laugh when I held the bow like a baseball bat. He didn't get impatient after reminding me for the hundredth time. "Yes, there *is* a difference between F and F#."

Now I am learning to create beautiful sounds. Sometimes they do not come together sounding remotely like the original song. And sometimes, I suspect, they may not sound so beautiful to everyone else. But, one day they will.

Musically, for now I am like the yogi, just "working my edge." One day I will complete my fantasy and sit in the garden making beautiful music on my cello. However, in the meantime, I have opted to be considerate of my neighbors and dream my impossible dream, but softly.

In our ongoing celebration of the "new" in our lives, Stan and I decided to expand the experience of Zen in the garden to include a six-week series of Zen workshops. This was an experience not to be forgotten.

The concept of Zen, according to some of the more esoteric writers, takes many, many pages to explain why it is not explainable. According to them, this is such an abstract concept that anyone who attempts to give you a short, concrete, definitive explanation of Zen should be ignored. For, by making the attempt, they have just proven that they don't know either.

Now, to establish my own limited knowledge base, I will do just that. "Zen," in my understanding, refers to an intensity of awareness. It means *really* being here *now*. This, at first, is no easy task. Good Westerners that we are, it is difficult for most of us to move from "doing" into just "being."

The experience of "being" is something that I have learned in the garden. It doesn't mean knowing all the botanical names of everything, or

making a list of all the garden tasks required. It means just experiencing and being in the moment as you walk through the garden. It means entering this space like a young child, who doesn't carry yesterday or tomorrow in with her, just the 'now,' *this* garden, *this* moment.

Ralph Waldo Emerson understood this when he looked at his roses and could behold them, just as they were, in that very moment.

> *The Roses under my window*
> *make no references to former*
> *roses or better ones; they are*
> *what they are; they exist*
> *with God today. There is no*
> *time to them. There is simply*
> *the rose; it is perfect in every*
> *moment of its existence.*

The Zen workshop focused on just this kind of awareness. Sitting in meditation, we concentrated on the stillness of being in the moment. Breathing in and breathing out slowly and aware of each breath, we gradually learned to bring a new mindfulness to breathing — and to being.

With each breath our bodies began to relax a bit more, and with the relaxation came a sense of peace. In time, and in this peaceful space, it become easier to let go of the hurts and angers in life, and to learn to offer them up. This is where forgiveness starts.

Like leaving the mountaintop, it was always a jolt to depart from the serenity of the Zen workshop and move into the rush of city traffic. After one of our last sessions we started the drive home in a mellow mood. As we drove through a busy intersection a speeding car suddenly shot out from a side street. With tires squealing and brakes screeching, he narrowly missed taking the front of our car with him as he accelerated again and sped off down the road.

"You stupid ass!" shouted Stan, adding a few loud, anatomically impossible suggestions to the now disappearing tail lights. Like I said, it takes time.

"Breathe in, breathe out," I suggested, with very poor timing.

"He's still an ass," added Stan, several moments later. "But, I forgive him for being an ass." Zen lives.

In future months, when we had similar encounters with other motorists, who also qualified for the "ass" description, I continued to share my sage advice to "offer it up," and to breathe in, breathe out." Then a funny thing happened. One day the dishwasher backed up and I responded to the resulting disaster with some extremely ripe words of my own.

"Breathe in, breathe out," suggested Stan, "just offer it up."

"That's really obnoxious," I thought, contemplating on how best to offer him up. So now I don't say that any more. Well, not much, anyway.

But, I just couldn't resist one more time. When the last wooden arch was erected over the entry to the secluded, raccoon path etched across the top beam was a reminder for us both. "Breathe in, Breathe Out."

Every time I walk through the "breathing arch" I am reminded once again, not just to breathe, but to be more aware to use these moments in the garden to be truly alive. Sometimes that just means to be still, to feel and to listen. I don't always listen too well, but when I do I have discovered that this is the process that opens the door to spiritual awareness.

I was listening one night a few years ago, when I had good reason to deal with my own fears of mortality. After spending several sleepless nights, I lay in bed one night just breathing slowly and, as I have so often advised others, offering it up.

There are no words to describe the stillness that followed. The deep peace I felt from within left no room for fear. The feeling was so immense that I knew that I had experienced something powerful. This was the same indefinable peace that I had once experienced many years before, when I realized that I had been touched by God.

An experience like this cannot be described in mere words. I used to laugh at John Wesley's words that his heart had been "strangely warmed." Now I don't laugh any more. I understand.

Theologians would call this the Paraclete, the presence of the Holy Spirit as Comforter. As for me, I don't need a fancy name for it I just call it another springtime in my life.

It is this same "morning" of springtime that the garden reminds us, is

once again, Eden. You can hear it in the words to my favorite hymn, "Morning Has Broken."

> *Sweet the rain's new fall sunlit from heaven,*
> *Like the first dew fall on the new grass.*
> *Praise for the sweetness of the wet garden,*
> *Sprung in completeness where God's feet pass.*
>
> *Mine is the sunlight! Mine is the morning*
> *Born of the one light Eden saw play!*
> *Praise with elation, praise every morning,*
> *God's re-creation of the new day!*
> —Eleanor Farjean, 1931, Presbyterian Hymnal

It is always a new day. This is the message of spring. And this is the message of the garden. It is not about endings. It is about new beginnings. We are always being born anew.

So that is my story. As the steward of my garden, I have nurtured it. And so, also, has the garden nurtured me.

# Alice's Garden Favorites

*Selected not for their uniqueness, but for beauty combined with hardiness and reliability.*

## TREES
*Blue Atlas Cedar* (Cedrus atlantica glauca), Weeping
*Canadian Hemlock* (Tsuga canadensis)
*Crabapple* (Malus floribunda) Red Jade
*Dogwood, Kousa* (Cornus Kousa)
*Heavenly Bamboo* (Nandina domestica)
*Holly* (Ilex)
    *American Holly* (Ilex opaca)
    *Foster Holly* (Ilex x attenuata)
    *Nellie Stevens Holly* (Ilex x Nellie R. Stevens)
*Japanese Andromeda* (Pieris japonica)
*Japanese Maple* (Acer japonicum)
*Japanese Snowbell* (Styrax japonica)
*Kwanzan Cherry* (Prunus serrulata kwanzan)
*Pine* (Pinus)
    *Japanese Black Pine* (Pinus thunbergii)
    *Skotch pine* (Pinus sylvestris)
*Redbud* (Cercis canadensis)
*Spruce* (Picea)
    *Colorado Blue Spruce* (Picea pungens glauca)
    *Norway Spruce* (Picea abies)

## SHRUBS
*Azalea* - all varieties
*Butterfly bush* (Buddleia)
*Crape Myrtle* (Lager stroemia indice)
*Hydrangea*
    *Annabelle* (Hydrangea arborescens)
    *Oakleaf* (Hydrangea quercifolia)
    *Panicle* (Hydrangea paniculata)
*Japanese Acuba* (Acuba japonica)

## SHRUBS cont.
*Laurel*
> *Cherry laurel* (Prunus laurocerasus)
> *Mountain laurel* (Kalmia latifolia)

*Rhododendron* (Roseum elegans)
*Spirea* (Spirea nipponica)
*Virburnum* (v. japonicum)
*Yew* (taxus)
> *Spreading English yew* (Taxus baccata)
> *Hicks Upright yew* (Taxus hicksii)

## FERNS
*Autumn fern* (Dryopteris erythosora)
*Christmas fern* (Polystichum acrostichoides)
*Japanese painted fern* (Athyrium niponicum pictum)
*Sword fern* (Polystichum munitum)
*Maidenhair fern* (Adiantum pedatum)

## GROUND COVER
*Allegheny spurge* (Pachysandra procumbens)
*Euonymous* (Euonymous fortuneii) "Emerald Gaiety"
*Lirope* (Lirope muscari) "Big Blue Lilyturf"
*Periwinkle* (Vinca minor)

## PERENNIALS
*Allium* (Alium angulosum)
*Astilbe* (X arendsii)
*Cleome* (Hassleriana)
*Columbine* (Aquilegia)
*Coreopsis* "Goldfink"
*Cranesbill* (Geraniacae) "Johnson blue geranium"
*Daffodil* (Narcissus)
*Daylily* (Hemerocallidaceae) "Stella d'oro"
*Dead Nettle* (Lanium)
*English bluebells* (Hyacintholdes non scripta)
*Foam flower* (Tiarella cordifolia)
*Heliopsis* (Heliopsis helianthoides) "Prairie Sunset"

## PERENNIALS cont.

*Hellebores* (Helleborous)
*Lenten Rose* (Helleborous orientalis)
*Christmas Rose* (Helleborous niger)
*Japanese Bleeding Heart* (Dicentra spectablis)
*Japanese Anemone* (Anemone x hybrida)
*Iris* (Iridaceae)
*Mountain Lilies* (Ixiolirion tataricum)
*Oriental Lily* (Lilium orientale)
*Peony* (Paeonia japonica)
*Pulmonaria* Lungwort (Boraginaceae) "Mrs. Moon"
*Purple coneflower* (Echinacea purpurea)
*Rose*
*Rudbeckia* "Black-eyed Susan"
*Spurge* (Euphorbia)
*Wild bleeding heart* (Diecentra eximia)
*Woodland Phlox* (Phlox divaricata)

## ANNUAL FLOWERS

*Ageratum*
*Begonias*
*Cosmos*
*Geranium*
*Impatiens*
*Marigold*
*Nicotiana*
*Petunia*
*Spider Lily* (Cleome)
*Sweet William*
*Zinnia*

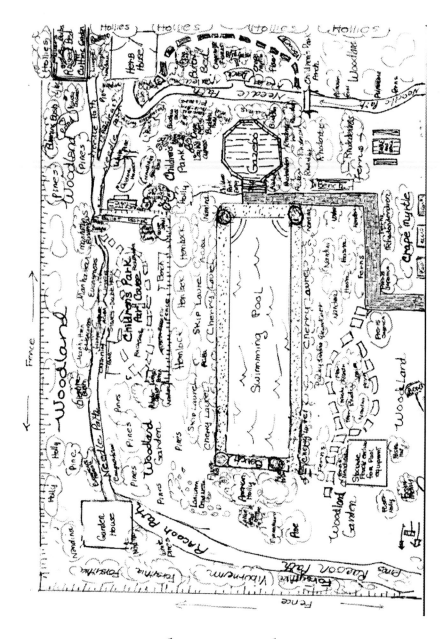

*Alice's Garden*

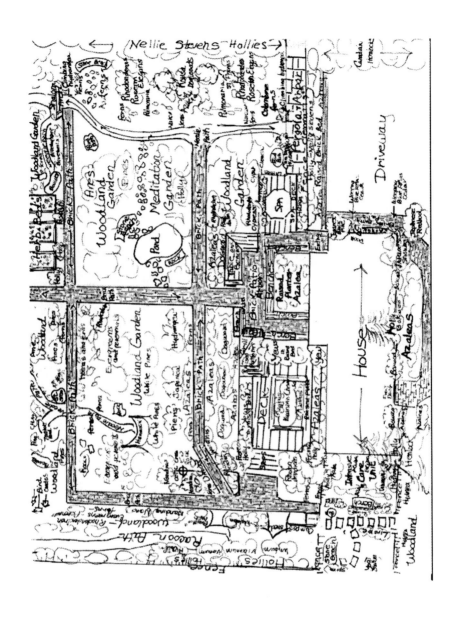

*Alice's Garden*

# ABOUT THE AUTHOR

Alice G. Miller, PhD, is a psychotherapist in private practice in Potomac, Maryland. She describes herself as a therapist by profession and a gardener by spirit.

A graduate of the University of Maryland School of Social Work, Dr. Miller is the author of three previous books. Prior to entering private practice, she has been the Director of a Youth Crisis Center, Director of a residential treatment program, and individual and family therapist with a psychiatric group practice.

Printed in the United States
65872LVS00003B/88-144

9 781596 637849